Mindfulness *in* Music

'Mark Tanner has written a mindfulness manifesto for music.'

BBC RADIO 3 'MUSIC MATTERS'

Mindfulness *in* Music

Notes on Finding Life's Rhythm

Mark Tanner

Leaping Hare Press

for Mum & Dad in the year of their Diamond Wedding Anniversary, 2018

First published in the UK in 2018 by
Leaping Hare Press
An imprint of The Quarto Group
The Old Brewery, 6 Blundell Street
London N7 9BH, United Kingdom
T (0)20 7700 6700 **F** (0)20 7700 8066
www.QuartoKnows.com

British Library Cataloguing-in-Publication Data
A catalogue record for this book is available from the British Library

ISBN: 978-1-78240-567-2

This book was conceived, designed and produced by
Leaping Hare Press
58 West Street, Brighton BN1 2RA, United Kingdom

Publisher SUSAN KELLY
Creative Director MICHAEL WHITEHEAD
Editorial Director TOM KITCH
Commissioning Editor MONICA PERDONI
Design & Art Direction WAYNE BLADES
Project Editor STEPHANIE EVANS
Illustrator MELVYN EVANS

Printed in China

3 5 7 9 10 8 6 4 2

Contents

INTRODUCTION

Music turns on our every breath.
It courses through our ears, our minds and our hearts, beating as fast as any trilling bird. Music lives in the tips of our fingers, but also on the tips of our tongues. Mindfulness and meditation resonate naturally with all forms of music, prompting us to listen with new ears and increase our receptiveness to beautiful sounds. Regardless of whether you are an avid music lover or a keen practitioner, a heightened awareness of music's organic qualities will open up an astonishing world of possibilities.

Mindfulness in Music

The essence of meditation is beautifully simple, yet Buddhists, who practise it for a lifetime, may still sense the possibility of a deeper, even more profound serenity. Similarly, a musician's longer-term pursuit of perfection will almost invariably be driven by a desire to achieve something immediate and personal.

In the broadest sense, exercising mindfulness in music is about being open, embracing and receptive to sound. Beyond this loose starting point, mindfulness splinters off into different directions according to our specific orientation. Being mindful as a performing musician, for example, means tapping into that most elusive of flow states, whereby one's musical expression is able to radiate outwards in a vivid, continuous stream. This requires the performer to be so at ease with the environment, and so focused on the musical experience itself, that nothing else – perhaps especially matters of execution (let alone the audience) – actually matters.

For the practising musician, who may have little or no aspiration ever to perform in public, but who prefers instead to derive pleasure from the act of playing or singing, mindfulness is about locking on to each valuable passing moment. This brings about more rewarding, satisfying playing and learning, and at the same time holds back the incapacitating habits of over-thinking, over-practising and over-reaching.

The act of doing should matter more to us than what we might eventually accomplish; when this is not the case, I can't help wondering if we are simply missing the point.

For the keen listener, mindfulness is primarily a matter of feeling free of distraction, so that one becomes entirely swept up by the music – or the dramatic sound of a storm thrusting its way through a valley, for example – and hence able to gain maximum pleasure from so doing. Equally, there will be times when it becomes important to play a more active role in the musical experience, not just sit back and allow the music to do all the work.

But irrespective of our orientation – which may well change over time – we will need to drill downwards into the nature of sound itself, not just our receptiveness to it, and perhaps also to contemplate afresh our own capacity for creativity.

Sweet Surrender

This all comes down to our willingness to surrender to music's intensity and poetry, and hence to relax our grip on our instinct to control it. How we think, how we breathe and how we physically move all influence our capacity to be nurtured by the music in our lives. Preconceptions about what music might have the potential to be will tend to distract us from what it actually is, right now. 'Here comes my favourite bit' is a common enough thought bubble when playing or listening to a piece we love, and yet it snatches from us any possibility of being moved by the particular verse, solo or middle-eight in full swing. Mindfulness gives full value to the immediate emotional impact of music – every appoggiatura, every unguarded crackle in the voice, every fleeting nuance – so that we find ourselves drawn further into the musical experience itself. Mindfulness in music leaves us with a feeling of equanimity, of self-balance. As we allow ourselves to be carried along on the crest of each musical wave, we are no longer swimming against the tide of our intellect; we steadily become more compassionate to ourselves, more in tune with those around us and more ready to imagine music as simply an extension of nature.

My Mindful Journey

My own mindful journey, I now realize, began even before I'd taken up the piano aged eight, the instrument that has since taken me all over the world many times, performing on land and at sea, examining, judging festivals and giving masterclasses. As a boy, I greatly enjoyed being on my own, thinking, reading, scheming, learning conjuring tricks from American magazines and giving in to the music that seemed to be underscoring my every move. I could lose myself for an hour at a time, staring out of a window, just watching the rain. The music that fired up my imagination at times became so loud and tempestuous that I recall being amazed my mother could not hear it coming out of my ears.

The assumptions we make when we are young about how other people's minds work tend to be amusingly off target. I assumed from as far back as I can remember that music was not just central to how humans interact with each other, but a defining quality of life itself. I also assumed that everybody aspires to play an instrument, at least to the level where they can play a dozen party pieces, and that listening to a new tune a couple of times is all anyone needs to be able to grab an instrument and play it back, or at least hum it. Few of these assumptions turned out to be remotely true, of course, and I suppose it was important for me to ease my way slowly into the real world, where there are as many views of what music is as there are people who are prepared to express one.

Every Breath You Take

As a college piano student, I spent a great deal of time studying scores and drinking coffee (in roughly equal measure). At first, I was a terrible practiser – I would shamble into a room, sit down and immediately launch into something difficult with which I might impress myself sufficiently to continue for a while longer. This self-induced shock tactic sometimes worked. But when it didn't, I lacked the resources with which to gain ground, mistaking engagement with sheer persistence. I suppose I thought of practice as 'work' and playing as 'play'; it was some time later that I realized the importance of gaining pleasure from every minute I was spending at the piano, whether at 'work' or not. My frame of mind when learning something new dictated whether I was 'doing battle' with it or exploring its inner personality. Things improved as I slowly came to terms with how quickly time passes and how easily opportunities seem to slip through our fingers; I began to explore my capacity to enjoy rather than endure the minutes and hours I was spending in the company of my instrument.

I was not a model student, or a particularly effective learner, yet a chance conversation with legendary pianist John Ogdon altered my approach overnight. He said to me, using the most sotto voce tone imaginable, 'Just because breathing has nothing to do with how pianists make their sound doesn't mean it has no effect on their ability to make *music*.' I pondered on this for some time – in fact, I still do – for this simplest of ideas achieves two vitally important things simultaneously: first, it helps to keep a pianist's body calm and the brain active; and second, it encourages them to think about the musical line rather than the means by which they are endeavouring to achieve it. I learned from Ogdon that we progress more effectively by avoiding binary 'black-and-white' thinking and going about things in a different, more thoughtful way. My practising gradually shifted from zealous fault-sifting to coaxing out the music waiting inside me. Once I'd learned to expect my favourite piano music to bounce around freely in my mind's ears, it quickly began to wrap itself around my other thoughts too, turning humdrum chores into mindful, sentient tasks.

BREATHING SPACE

In mindfulness, our every breath beckons us closer to an inner sanctuary: the one place we can truly call our own. Mindfulness and breathing make ideal bedfellows simply because, apart from blinking (which of course ceases the moment we close our eyes), breathing is the one thing we are always subliminally aware our bodies are doing, even when at rest. Ideally, mindful breathing will begin amid an oasis of tranquillity, free from Twitter feeds and pinging microwaves. Eventually, once we have learned to just 'be' in the present moment, we can experiment with noisier environments. We may later choose to use music to accompany our meditation, though this can at first prove challenging, for music almost invariably asserts its own agenda. It occurs to me we often present music *to* our ears in expectation of some sort of response; paradoxically, it is only when we allow ourselves to breathe *with* the music that our experience can become a mindful one. And yet, importantly, mindfulness is not just about achieving a state of inner calm; it is also about increasing our stimulation and insight, and these are things music can help foster.

An important first step is simply to notice what you are experiencing. If you are lying in a field, notice each bee that buzzes overhead; or if you are riding in the back of a cab, close your eyes, acknowledge each burst of radio-babble and relish the peace in your head. Ride each wave of sound until you become aware another has begun to drift in your direction. Focusing on the breathing itself – regular and long, moment by moment – will keep you from becoming overwhelmed by sound, however musical or unmusical it may appear to be.

Be a Child Again

Many of the exercises and ideas in this book spring naturally out of my own early, gloriously naive experiences with sound – not exclusively music, I should add – and also my teaching, which has done much to shape my approach to engaging with music on many different levels. Meditation was, now that I reflect upon my rain watching and symphonic head explosions, always an intrinsic component. It also strikes me, as a non-Buddhist agnostic, that many of our adult ambitions for calmness, living in the moment and being kind to ourselves often come more easily to children. Our quest, therefore, is perhaps not so much a matter of discovering a new 'us' as reconnecting with the old one. For it is our preoccupation with 'why' and 'how' that has incipiently stolen from us our capacity for just 'being', and allowing ourselves to live non-judgementally from day to day.

Now that I have allowed music to seep into every corner of my existence, I feel I have something worth sharing. When I sit on the sun deck of a cruise ship, composing a piece that will eventually find its way into some publication or other, I am also striving to be aware of cloud shapes or shadow patterns, and wondering how they might somehow influence my music. When I am learning or relearning a piano piece, I am continually reminding myself what it was about it that first fired me up. When I am teaching, examining or adjudicating, I try to keep in mind what it felt like to be that small person with lots to say but little facility with which to say it. When I am performing, I aim to be the most attentive member of my audience, and when I am writing I do my best to express the emotional basis of my knowledge. The joy of writing this book, perched on crumbling walls in Turkey with an iPad and a double cappuccino, is all the more meaningful for me as I dare to contemplate you reading it and threading bits and pieces from it into your own life, irrespective of the role music and mindfulness currently play within it.

MUSIC IS NOT JUST FOR MUSICIANS

My ambition for this book is to help connect the world we all share with the private world we inhabit alone in our heads. After all, meditation is not solely the province of Buddhists, and by the same token, music is not just for musicians.

THERE IS NO IMPLICATION of the need to become an expert, either in music or mindfulness for that matter, just a gentle suggestion that we could weigh up our options with a little greater care. Music provides the ideal interface between mindfulness and the practicalities that intrude upon our daily lives: for the proficient singer or instrumentalist music binds together the creative and meditative senses, while for the music lover it may provide the perfect foil for stress. For all of us, music contributes to a kind of photo album captured in colourful snippets of sound, punctuating the highs and underscoring the lows; it joins up the dots of our oldest memories and adds to an ongoing timeline that will probably make rather better sense a decade on. Music teases out thoughts we never would have known we are capable of, and bonds us ever more tightly to those with whom we feel an especial kinship. It is the shared currency of music that defines its humanity, and yet virtually any sound can acquire the status of beautiful – the aquatic fizz of an incoming tide at sunset takes on a whole new charm when we stand hand in hand with a loved one. While some of us choose to commune with fellow singers in a choral society, one can just as easily commune with a dawn chorus, simply by being there and taking notice.

Exercising mindfulness is as hard or as easy as we choose to make it – on one level, we can simply strive to be a little calmer, more aware of how we spend our leisure time, and less inclined to wish our lives away when sitting at our work desk; on another level, we can evolve a whole new mindset and perhaps even alter the course of our lives. For all of us there will inevitably be times when we find ourselves drifting

'I often think in music. I live my daydreams in music. I see my life in terms of music.'

Albert Einstein (1879–1955)
German-born theoretical physicist

TAKE THE PLUNGE

When you go to the swimming baths, do you generally consider yourself to be a plunger or a toe-dipper? Chances are, if you're as fickle as me, your strategy will reflect your current level of inner confidence (and also how chilly the changing room is). Perhaps something similar occurs when we are choosing what music to listen to? Certainly, we cannot always be ready to split the musical atom. Sometimes we just need to wallow in the familiar, but at other times we could challenge ourselves to be more enterprising in our choice – not to 'stretch' ourselves just for the sake of it, but simply to keep open the possibility of discovering something entirely new and wonderful. We should permit ourselves a smile each time we add a new piece to our pleasure bank, just as we ought to be pleasantly surprised we took the plunge and leapt elegantly – and in slow motion, like a polar bear – into the deep end of the swimming pool.

into an automaton mode whereby mindfulness gives way to spells of mindlessness. But this merely confirms the need for a more decisive, consistent approach – both to the role music plays in our lives and to the value we place on our overall state of mind. There is nothing chimerical or flimsy about the notion of becoming more mindful; in fact, we begin to achieve it simply by being more purposeful, channelled and time savvy. Aside from our physical health, there can be little else more important to our long-term well-being.

Music's Elevating Qualities

Though music's uplifting qualities are undeniable, in the twenty-first century we might be just as likely to experience music in the form of a rude encounter in an elevator. This has even prompted pessimists to remark that we risk sliding into a state of spiritual deficit. The most troubling by-product of so-called 'muzak' is that we have no say in whether we experience it; the choice is to tolerate it or attempt to block it out, but not to turn it off. For some, the scourge of noise pollution has become a perennial preoccupation, for peace and tranquillity can no longer be counted upon as the default. Music only becomes transformative and nurturing when we are permitted to encounter it on our own terms. Hence, deciding *when* to invite music inside us has become as important as choosing the poetic form it might take. Perhaps, as a consequence, we are in danger as a society of losing our capacity to think of music as a precious, extraordinary gift.

Cynics would say we treat music increasingly as a buy-one-get-one-free commodity. The word 'music', after all, comes from 'muses' – the daughters of Zeus – to crystallize the purest conceivable artistic aspirations of the gods. If we allow our thoughts to drift back to ancient times, when music mirrored the firmament first and fulfilled workaday functions second, we see how far our expectations have gradually shifted. Among music's many attributes is its authority to pose challenging questions about life and death, rather than to

> 'Music with dinner is an insult both to
> the cook and the violinist.'
>
> G. K. CHESTERTON (1874–1936)
> ENGLISH WRITER AND PHILOSOPHER

present easy answers. Despite what the American rock band Aerosmith would have us believe, finding love in an elevator is about as likely as encountering music you might actually be in the mood to listen to.

Listening with Renewed Purpose

We encounter music increasingly randomly these days. Indeed, our capacity to take for granted any beautiful sound, be it from a bird, bonfire or violin, may at times outstrip our willingness to give it a fair hearing. To listen passively is to barely notice, and ultimately to damn with faint praise. Importantly, we should distinguish between passive listening in everyday life – indifferent, supine, uncaring even – and the active decision to listen non-judgementally that is a prerequisite for mindfulness. The child who has just finished practising her clarinet thoughtfully in an adjacent room deserves something more than a half-hearted comment along the lines of 'that sounded nice, dear'. But to be capable of a more meaningful reflection presupposes we have been listening with some degree of attentiveness. It falls upon us to praise the glimpses of spontaneity creeping into the child's playing, or her slightly improved intonation perhaps, for it is these gently nurturing observations that will keep the child's boat afloat. Her ambition to please you is where her own mindful journey may conceivably begin; the two of you could one day be walking the same stretch of road.

Though most of us consider ourselves to be observant, I am quietly convinced we take in our surroundings chiefly with our eyes, and partly through our sense of smell; our ears are often just reluctant appendages, or convenient places to hook our spectacles. We may hear, but are we really listening? Our hearing has considerable bandwidth, yet it does not often occur to us to tune in; like our best tablecloth, we tend to save it for special occasions.

Moreover, we have become far more difficult to please. Surely not all music needs to be of the highest quality before it is capable of rewarding a moment's attention? It is easy to dismiss a subway busker's earnest attempts at a cover song if it fails to meet with expectations (indeed, the media's fascination with competition may possibly have squeezed out our last drops of generosity in this regard). Music, in whatever forms we most readily resonate with it, remains an incomparably rich human resource – and yet, to be touched we need to be touchable. A willingness to be receptive goes hand in hand with a kind of vulnerability – the risk of hearing something that displeases or troubles us, perhaps. It may even seem at times that such openness comes at too high a price. One occasionally comes across accomplished musicians who seem to feel that, in applauding the musical efforts of others, something has been taken away from *them* – someone else's gain equals their loss. Music examiners need to be especially on their guard in this respect. They may have pens in their hands, but they are still an audience to a performance; each performance makes its mark, albeit briefly, and then makes space for the next one.

Listening with purpose is not just about according dignity to someone (or something) else, it is how we embrace each passing moment and delight in what it is to be alive. Even if we feel lukewarm at the sound of a certain musical instrument, perhaps we can find it in our hearts to chime with the human being who invested so much of themselves into playing it. Sound, and by extension music, can act as an ideal conduit to our sensuality; it can also span the chasm between intellect and emotion as we endeavour to make sense of what, and why, we feel what we feel. If your postman's whistle happens to be particularly tuneful tomorrow morning, it will cost you nothing to smile by way of encouragement.

Become a Virtuoso Listener

Before we can find more in the music we love, or begin to explore the prospect of fulfilment in less familiar music, our ears need cultivating to the next level of engagement. In my book, *The Mindful Pianist* (2016), I challenged the reader to aspire to the level of 'virtuoso listener' by first paying close attention to the ordinary, then the less ordinary, and ultimately the extraordinary. Only then will the question of *what* we listen to become more relevant. In this introductory chapter I have chosen to segue freely between considering the sensation of natural sound – the music of our environment – and man-made sound, which often depends for its impact upon the sophisticated manipulations of form and content, technique and craftsmanship. It seems we are largely reliant upon patterns and other convenient markers in order to sustain our level of concentration on sound. But lapses in

PEEL THE MUSICAL ONION

When we peel an onion, we have before us nature's prototype Russian doll; concentric circles of crisp white flesh, each fiercely protecting the layer next to it. We keep peeling and, if we happen to be listening to a piece of music as we work, we begin to notice new elements, one by one. We are not trying to be profound, or insightful; we are just noticing the layers of meaning bound up in the music, rather as they appear bound up in the onion. If we listen hard enough, perhaps we will notice something in the music we had not spotted before – a strangely beautiful solo instrument cutting through the 'middle' of the sound; an echoey rush of stratospheric notes; the pleasant throb of a bass guitar.

concentration are by no means solely a hazard for practising musicians. For although the magic of music is stirred into life by the composer and performer, the listener is no less vital a link, albeit some way further along the creative chain. When listeners lose their point of focus, the spell is broken, and all the energy distilled in the music is squandered. The key to retaining focus is to engage with music creatively, not passively. This could mean listening for something new each time a particular piece is heard, using the shuffle mode of your playback device to gain practice at listening to it out of sequence, or, when appropriate, getting hold of different versions of the same piece to keep up your interest.

MUSIC IN THE MOMENT

Our fidgeting minds often prove to be even more distracting than the person sitting next to us, humming arrhythmically or chewing gum. Mindfulness quickly draws us back to the source of the sound: the source of the pleasure itself.

IN LIVE MUSIC SETTINGS, a whole range of potential distractions are there to limit our enjoyment if we allow them to. It can be helpful to focus on something other than the obvious when we sense that our concentration has begun to wander. Most of us unwittingly home in, for example, on the hands or head of a pianist, the eyes and mouth of a singer, or the upper body movements of a conductor. But if we consciously focus elsewhere, for example the pianist's feet or the singer's hands, we might find our ears quickly return to the music. Do we really need our eyes open at all? If we have a printed programme in our hands, as is the norm for classical concerts, this easily becomes the biggest distraction of all – we may miss an exquisite cor anglais solo because we have become distracted by the programme note writer's insights, or worse still, find ourselves unaccountably absorbed by some random advert for draught excluders. In a folk, jazz or similar setting, we could try to fix our gaze on a member of the group who we might not normally be as interested in, or perhaps home in on the visual communication happening between those musicians who are not at that moment performing a solo. You might try focusing on a single wall tile or roof rafter; we become more creative, and thereby more attentive, when we look away, not when we stare fixedly. These are just a few basic but potentially useful tools for countering distraction.

We become more creative, and thereby more attentive, when we look away, not when we stare fixedly

Some listeners enjoy imagining they are performing when they hear a piece played exquisitely well – the heavy rocker's 'air guitar' springs to mind – or picture themselves in some far-flung place that fits with a particular scene the music was

OPEN THE GATES TO YOUR MIND PALACE

The next time you visit a medieval city, head for a busy market place, make a point of standing alone on the cobbles with your eyes closed – and simply listen. From amid all the hustle-bustle, the city may be willing to give up one of its cherished secrets.

intended to invoke. There is, of course, never an obligation to go along with a proposed narrative or backdrop to a piece, however evocative its title. If it suits you to think of Nina Simone's 'I Get Along Without You Very Well' (by far my personal favourite cover version of Hoagy Carmichael's 1939 song) as laconic rather than ironic, so be it; neither Carmichael's nor Simone's opinion of you will ever come into it. Challenging yourself with new music by a composer, band or solo performer whose output you have enjoyed before is also a good way to boost concentration, as is following a score of the piece if you happen to be able to read notation pretty well.

We can choose whether to place our ears on standby mode or to become more alert to the subtle potency of sound. Mindful listening and purposeful listening will dovetail in subtly different ways according to the needs of the moment. This could mean being attentive to the smallest variants in texture and hue – the aural equivalent to the care over detail shown by an accomplished watercolour artist. If a beautiful sound is miraculous, our ability to instantly know it for what it is seems equally so. The smallest child can detect with impressive accuracy from how far away an ice-cream van is approaching. I find I can still tell the difference between a Kawasaki, Honda or Harley-Davidson motorcycle just from the throatiness of its engine, even from several blocks away – a throwback to my teenage years, riding heroically and leather-clad through the back roads of my home town.

Music & the Power of Concentration

We all need to be able to concentrate as we go about our daily lives; paradoxically, however, while for some of us music provides the ideal way to relax and restore concentration, for others it may actually appear to be the problem itself. Even the most celebrated musicians unaccountably lose confidence in their own ability to concentrate on the job in hand, which can lead to the sudden onset of nerves. For example, the Russian pianist Vladimir Horowitz experienced pre-recital jitters to such an extent that well-wishers often had to physically drag him on stage. Once nerves become the driver, concentration quickly becomes a twitchy passenger.

A musician's concentration needs to be sufficiently robust to shrug off the odd intrusive door squeak, and you may be surprised to read of one well-known performer's idiosyncratic solution. The American pianist Glenn Gould was able to evolve a cunning strategy, of sorts, to the problem of concentration. Actually, it arose in his early teens quite by accident when practising a fiendishly difficult passage by Mozart – a vacuum cleaner spontaneously leapt into life nearby and initially took him by surprise. He persisted playing nevertheless and, to his pleasant surprise, found he actually preferred the sound of his mechanical practising when partly smothered by the uncompromising din of the machine. In fact, he would later deliberately recreate the effect of the vacuum cleaner by forcing himself to work at the piano with TV Westerns and random rock music blaring in the background. Gould's solution might seem a little abstruse, but the point is that it evidently worked for him.

Gould's experience should encourage us to think outside the box a little and perhaps attempt something similar for ourselves in order to re-establish concentration. As a teenager I worked for a time in a busy butcher's shop with a school friend. The boss was an inveterate practical joker who took pleasure in frightening the living daylights out of us by creeping up behind us and dropping an empty aluminium meat tray onto the concrete floor. Though I was never fully able to come to terms with these ear-splitting crashes, I did gradually become better at

If a beautiful sound is miraculous, our ability to instantly know it for what it is seems equally so

'Music is like a dream. One that I cannot hear.'

LUDWIG VAN BEETHOVEN (1770–1827)
GERMAN COMPOSER AND PIANIST

making instantaneous adjustments to my reactions. I have even been known to use a fusion of Gould's method and my own 'sudden crash' scenario when preparing music students for pressure situations, such as exams, auditions or performances. What doesn't kill us makes us stronger.

Finding Beauty in Natural Sound

The relationship between mindfulness and music becomes all the more palpable if we just stop for a brief moment now and again, and listen with the intensity of concentration an owl brings to its nocturnal adventures. There is beauty to enjoy in our everyday musical experiences, no matter how fleeting or seemingly trivial. There is also much to be enticed by in the ambient sound of our surroundings. If a blind person happened to be present during a bank robbery, she would in all probability be able to supply a significant amount of invaluable information over and above the sighted witnesses – details such as accents and ages, subtleties of hierarchy within the gang or irregularities of walking pattern, much of which may not even occur to the rest of us. Learning to use what we have to the best advantage is how we flourish.

Though there are times when it makes perfect sense to ram our fingers into our ears, I doubt any one of us would zone out of our vivid soundworld as routinely as we do if we were to dare to imagine what it might be like to suddenly become deaf. Beethoven's hearing loss, which became progressive until his forties (by which point his hearing had disappeared altogether), undoubtedly opened up his mind's ears even more acutely than before – he went on to compose the *Missa Solemnis* and *Choral* symphony with zero hearing. Just imagine having an inner ear of such dependable quality. And yet I would wager Beethoven would have prized the sound of a blackbird as highly as any virtuoso by the end of his life.

As I write this I am browsing absent-mindedly through a set of recital programmes for the following week as I prepare to board the *Queen Victoria*, having just touched down in Santiago, Chile. The hotel air-conditioning unit began attention-seeking an hour ago, but has since settled itself into a fantastically rhythmic ostinato strangely reminiscent of Ravel's *Bolero*, tinged with a weird strain of acid jazz. These oddly insistent pulsations will probably pop back into my mind a dozen times before we've even sailed away. Peculiar experiences such as this remind me that beauty is in the ear of the beholder; the key to discovering our musical world afresh is simply to keep our ears switched on and remain open to the possibility of something new.

CHAPTER ONE

MUSIC AS MEDITATION

Music's meditative qualities are awe-inspiring. By whatever definition of spirituality one can imagine, music has always played an intrinsic part, perhaps through collective worship in a church, monastery or mosque, or at home alone, sitting peacefully, devoid of any religious connotation whatsoever. For the listener, music draws us into the space we have set aside for our own personal meditation – and for the musician, music eventually becomes a sort of practical meditation. Music and meditation help us to slip from physical space into mental space; we find ourselves transported into a different kind of reality.

Seeing the Wood for the Trees

Mindfulness in music simply means feeling it, soaking it up, chiming with its impulses and lingering for breath at its natural places of repose. Importantly, understanding music rarely requires analysis. If we love a piece, or detest it, we understand it well enough to know whether we might listen to it again.

There is never any need for us to feel that we lack what it takes to grasp what makes a piece of music 'tick'. For no matter how sprawling or impressive music's outward appearance may be, there is nothing to be understood, unless, of course, one later develops a fascination for a particular piece of music's intricate machinery. But even then, I contend it is our musical vocabulary that will have been intrigued, or perhaps our sense of historical inquisitiveness – not our emotional receptivity, for that was there already, confidently rooted inside us. It is often said that a little knowledge can be dangerous. By extension, in music there can actually be times when an *excess* of knowledge halts a listener completely in her tracks; the music's innocent charm slips tantalizingly out of reach. An ability to listen carefully but non-judgementally is perhaps one of the hardest things we can ask of ourselves.

Intricate music is a little like a Swiss clock – just as beautiful on the inside as it is on the outside. And yet, many of us never become remotely interested in how music functions beneath its surface. Why should a profound love of music have anything to do with deciphering those mysterious black dots scattered on manuscript paper, or knowing what inspired Dave Brubeck to write 'Take Five'? After all, an ability to speak does not presuppose an ability to read words, any more than an ability to enjoy an expertly prepared meal presupposes our own capacity to cook like a gourmet. For the avid musician or aficionado, details of this sort may gradually become woven into the fabric of a particular work, whereas for the enthusiastic music lover such things could possibly seem about as riveting as a washing-machine manual. There is perhaps no better illustration of the concept of emotional intelligence versus intellectual intelligence than a comparison of a dozen people's reactions to the same piece of music. It stands to reason that we will all seek out something different in the music we love; hence no single approach can be viewed as superior to any other. We can only truly hear what we are minded to hear, what our ears and hearts are ready to drink in at that particular moment. Let that be sufficient, at least for the time being.

The Windmills of Your Mind

Exercising mindfulness each day seems a little like gardening: it is never truly complete, but ongoing and gratifyingly impermanent. What's more, though music is sometimes sculpted down to the briefest snippet, it too can appear unending; we could lose ourselves just as easily in a four-minute pop song as a four-hour opera. In music, as in meditation, the objective is not to get it 'done', but to lose ourselves in the act of *doing* it; the passing of time itself becomes of little importance. Like a windmill, we simply allow our emotions to catch the breeze.

A recurring theme of this book is the potential for any form of beautiful sound – be it an Intermezzo by Brahms, a remix of 'Cry Me a River' or a distant roll of thunder – to reaffirm our personality and humanity in ways even our closest soulmates could never achieve. Leaving to one side the fact that our words tend to leave much unsaid, music has the power to

DRINK IN YOUR SURROUNDINGS

The next time you find yourself in some woodland, headphones snugly in place, permit yourself to feel that the music you are listening to is yours and yours alone. For at that exact moment there may well be no other human being in the world who is engaged in such a relationship with that particular chorus, riff or climax. As you saunter through the dewy grass and slowly begin to drink in your surroundings, you are not tuning in to the music passively, but listening attentively, and with the emotional intelligence of any seasoned conductor.

My listening suggestions are Alan Hovhaness's *Spirit of Trees*, Toru Takemitsu's *From Me Flows What You Call Time*, and the album by Yes, *Tales from Topographic Oceans*.

recalibrate our expectations and at the same time help us to make better sense of our complex lives. It is not important to know why we yearn to hear something, though admittedly the better we know how the music goes, the greater its potential to assist with meditation; we may feel less inclined to interrogate it, more willing to just let it wash over us. Besides, our choice of music may not be as random as we imagine, for a familiar melody can sometimes underscore an emotion we had not even realized we were in the midst of experiencing. We love our favourite music for what it is able to reveal to us about itself, but also for its power to tease out sensations we wish to revisit.

Music – Past, Present & Future

Music connects us to our past and holds a spotlight to our present. Nostalgia is among music's non-negotiable facets, for as soon as we form a preference for a particular song or piece of music, the nostalgia ball starts rolling.

Nostalgic music is like a comfort blanket that wraps itself around us ever more tightly as we grow older, giving orientation and focus to the person we have since become. Like a dog-eared sepia photograph dusted off from a recently rediscovered box in the attic, we instantly recognize the aroma of our musical past. Nostalgic moments are not evidence of us slackening our grip on reality, but a welcome boost to our morale and a reaffirmation of the space from which our courage and fortitude took root. The first little tune we learned on the trumpet, or the record that was playing when we sneaked our first kiss, are grains in the sands of our time on this earth. We can of course experience vicarious nostalgia, too – the sense of something historically meaningful that was never actually a part of our own lives but which may have played a significant part in a loved one's. Younger folk may take a certain pleasure, for example, in seeing that Vera Lynn reached her hundredth year, knowing how important 'We'll Meet Again' must have been for countless war veterans.

Those who remain adamant that familiarity breeds contempt are probably underplaying their own need to revisit the music that once touched their souls. Granted, it may help us, at times, to be a little thick-skinned, but there is surely no virtue in being impenetrable. Nor do we need to feel embarrassed about the music we once loved; it is not an indictment, simply a memento. Besides, an unwillingness to acknowledge where we have come from suggests an alarming incapacity to reflect, let alone stargaze. Just as we hanker for comfort food from time to time – for me, it's scrambled eggs or mashed potatoes – we should all be proud to hold a privileged backstage pass to our musical histories. The past is all ours, despite the inevitable intersecting circles of our teenage years. And yet our past does not define who we were then, or who we are today. Musical nostalgia is not about naivety, but a sense of belonging and ownership of our past; nostalgia is also about allowing ourselves to relive important moments, on rainy days and sunny ones too.

Musical Memorabilia

Listening to BBC Radio 4's *Desert Island Discs*, I heard Kirsty Young interviewing Marian Keyes, the Irish novelist, who was born the same year as me, 1963. One of her choices was Petula Clark's 'Downtown', an unstoppably optimistic melody that always catches my attention like a whiff of Swinging Sixties' perfume. I remember bopping about to the record as a small child; the instant I hear it these days, I am back in my parents' lounge, clutching an imaginary microphone. Our slowly increasing need to reconnect with the music of yesteryear perhaps tells us something uncomfortable about our current state of mind – for once we reach our fifties, most of us will already have lived more than half of our lives, so it stands to reason we will gradually become more fond, in some cases preoccupied, with our earlier tastes, accomplishments, loves and losses.

Curiously, though, when most of us talk about nostalgia in reference to music, we mean pop, jazz, or one of its spin-offs/ derivatives. Arguably, anyone who loves classical music (by which most of us are referring to 'serious' Western music spanning the past three or four centuries) is almost compelled

More Time to Live, More Time to Listen

According to a piece of research undertaken for the *Guardian* newspaper, life expectancy in the UK currently increases by five hours every day. What will you do with yours? Just think of the music you might listen to, the time you could invest in taking up a new instrument, or simply sitting quietly in the garden with a cup of tea and a melodious song thrush to entertain you.

to be nostalgic. And yet, paradoxically, Debussy, a composer who died in 1918, tends still to be labelled 'classical' in record stores and 'modern' by those who have yet to connect confidently with the contemporary scene. The phrase 'all the best composers are dead' is used so flippantly these days that we could easily overlook the existence of the contemporary English composer Mark-Anthony Turnage or the American John Luther Adams – for some, their music is yet to be discovered, while for others it is already sufficiently familiar to be dubbed nostalgic.

But nostalgia is by no means a modern-day phenomenon. There are numerous examples of composers and performers who borrowed from the past, revered it or memorialized it, well before Mendelssohn, without whom much of J. S. Bach's music may have languished forgotten in Weimar for eternity.

Rachmaninov was an arch-Romantic who largely resisted the cutting-edge ideologies sported by Stravinsky and other luminaries of his day in favour of what he felt he understood best. Any musician who is reluctant to distance himself from history is setting himself up to be unfairly dismissed as démodé by the current or subsequent generation. But we cannot turn off our nostalgic inclinations at will, and nor should we wish to; the sounds of our past may be distant, but they are all the more powerful because of that.

As Time Goes By

Listening to jazz, blues and folk can give us the misleading impression of music not so much fixed in a particular point in time as eternally perennial. In each case the capacity for reinvention may seem so infinite, and the pathways forwards and backwards so crowded with hybrids and fusion styles, that we might even suppose they never had 'roots' at all. How can we disentangle folk traditions from the music of Bob Dylan or Fleetwood Mac, let alone gospel and blues from Adele? The ephemeral nature of pop music perhaps goes some way to explaining its built-in time bomb – though sometimes a time bomb with a miraculously long fuse wire, for the best pop music usually endures for long enough to effectively smooth over the crack between Generation X and Generation Y. Presumably this explains the ongoing popularity of tribute bands. The term 'disposable' when applied to pop music carries with it a sense of being replaceable – we can peg it as disposable if we wish, but only because we secretly know where we can find it when we need it; pop music is surely more than fast food for the ears. For many, young and old, each seasonal reincarnation of Slade's raucously festive classic, 'Merry Christmas', signals another year that has passed by with alarming alacrity; but whether we loathe the record or love it, we have no right to deny its right to exist.

In truth, a reluctance to let go of the past tells us nothing about our willingness to spring forwards confidently into our unknown futures. Nostalgia is by no means a failing of the timid-hearted or unambitious. My friend Paul da Vinci, lead singer of The Rubettes, a group that produced timeless songs such as 'Sugar Baby Love', is now in his sixties – he remains as youthfully optimistic about the future as ever, now composing 'classical' music as well as great pop songs; at the same time, he remains justifiably proud of his past. As time trickles by, we all accumulate more and more musical memorabilia: the present slips backwards, and the past slips back further

'I've always said that pop music is disposable ...
If it wasn't disposable it'd be a pain in the fuckin' arse.'

Elton John (1947–)
ENGLISH SINGER, PIANIST AND COMPOSER,
QUOTED IN *A DICTIONARY OF MUSICAL QUOTATIONS*

still. Though the music of our personal futures is of course unknown, we can be confident that nostalgia will continue to rely upon the thought connections we are making right now with certain songs or pieces of music. Any of the reinvention we flatter ourselves that we have managed along the way comes as a direct response to the past, and hence is forever indebted to it. None of us was born in a time warp; nor, for that matter, was the music we grew up with.

Reclaiming the Peace in Our Heads

Most of us have an inner critic, a miscreant creature skulking around in our heads, intent on providing a running commentary on our failings. The extent to which we become enslaved by it, beholden to its hollow praise or intimidated by its superficial authority, becomes the all-important question.

For as long as I can remember, music has consumed a considerable part of my head space. It is as if some crazy-haired composer's alter ego took up squatters' rights in my mind at the age of eight and has since refused to budge. I sometimes wonder if my fingers came pre-installed with piano music, too; for like headless chickens, they twitch away at the kitchen table in response to unexplained musical urges. And yet, I find there is something strangely cathartic to be gained from allowing myself to act out the music that spontaneously

CONNECT THE BRAINWAVES TO YOUR HEART

An ability to access a piece of music you know well – to pluck it from your memory at will – is to be highly prized. Imagine being able to call upon your entire iTunes library just by mentally dialling up what you wish to hear and pressing 'play'. A good way to start is to take a piece or song you know really well and listen to it while physically present in several different environments – for example, on a cliff walk, in the bath or on a coastal train journey. By triangulating your emotional responses to the music, you effectively connect what the contemporary musicologist John Sloboda called 'the brainwaves to your heart'. From here, the ambient beauty of the music and the strong associations you have etched into your memory become indispensable touchpoints; they may eventually become part of the musical experience itself.

turns over in my mind. I came to terms with these involuntary gesticulations long ago, for they mean me no harm.

As a concert pianist, I am all too aware of the pressure to memorize lengthy, complex pieces of music and regurgitate them on demand. I have spent thousands of hours patiently refining this skill over the years; the drip, drip, drip of intricate details melting into sound-soaked grey cells. One lives with the uneasy reality that the million notes carefully stashed away may start to dribble out again – surely the sponge must become saturated at some point? Perhaps you

Savouring the Here and Now

When we allow mindfulness to steer us in some tangible direction, especially perhaps through the medium of music, something rather miraculous happens: we find ourselves letting go of injurious thoughts by replacing them with decisive actions. Like a thermostat that has been preset to restore balance and order, we are shaken back into the present moment. This, in turn, serves to instantly refuel our creative impulses; and so the positive cycle turns steadily forwards. When music's transformative energy is permitted to flow, it gushes like a mountain stream through the mind, tempering it in a radiant wash of colour and leaving its course clear of obstacles.

For many people, meditation is to music as food is to the soul; each seems utterly inextricable from the other. But the wonderment captured in a tiny act of musical creativity can only occur when the mind and body are freed from encumbrances, just as is achieved when meditating. And by creativity, I mean listening, or playing music quietly to oneself perhaps, not necessarily giving a virtuoso performance to a packed hall; there is, after all, no especial virtue to virtuosity *per se*. Thought of in this way, mindfulness in music suddenly permits many things to become distinctly possible. The important thing to keep in mind is that 'now' all too quickly becomes 'then'. We need to savour the moment before it evaporates into the ether.

have experienced the fear of encountering a mental blank as you arrive at the punchline in your best-man's speech, or stumbling maddeningly when repeating your own wedding vows? Classical pianists face the prospect of heart-in-mouth experiences every time they stride out on to a dimly lit stage and sit down to play for ninety minutes without a scrap of music in sight. The upshot of all this is that performing musicians, and indeed others who take their playing seriously, become prone to over-practising in a groundhog-day bid to prove to themselves they've still got all those bits of information safely banked away. Use it or lose it. In a sense, every new piece added to our heads challenges the peace in our heads.

Like many other musicians, my epiphanic moment came much later, by which point I had instinctively begun to inch away from the pressure of performing in prominent venues. Instead of stretching my memory to breaking point, I resolved to give it a good flushing out from time to time; I would also place fewer obstacles in my own path and go about my musical life in a more mindful way. I now realized that playing with the sheet music in front of me wasn't a cop-out after all – in fact, it instantaneously made available to me whole tranches of challenging contemporary repertoire that I may never have dared to perform in public otherwise. It also meant learning to mentally breathe out and allow my head to slow down to a canter from time to time. Being generous to myself turned out to be my most indispensable self-taught piano lesson.

Stuck On You

Music can easily take over our heads if we permit it to; a chorus from a tune we don't even like all too easily becomes compulsive, distracting and energy-draining. Fortunately, it turns out we have the tools to halt unwanted music in its tracks. A study by Dr Kelly Jakubowski of Durham University in the UK showed that there are a few constructive things we might try if an 'earworm' (persistent melody) is proving especially irksome to block out from the mind.

WHEEDLE OUT THE EARWORMS

1. Listen all the way through the tune: This can effectively smother it out in one fell swoop, since it is likely that only the tune's catchier moments will prove problematic to shift.
2. Go for a full system-erase: We may be able to successfully wheedle out the earworm by listening (or playing) through a completely different piece. This will hopefully have the effect of wiping away the offending gremlin. According to Jakubowski, 'God Save the Queen' scored highest in her survey of potent earworm busters!
3. Keep the cogs whirring: A disengaged brain is apparently more prone to the onset of earworms, so why not try reactivating it with, say, a sudoku puzzle, or even by washing the dishes?
4. Sing the offending tune backwards: This is my own mindful solution – I simply start at its last note and work steadily backwards, note by note (or word by word), until I arrive at the start. It's a bit like wiping a blackboard clean.

SELF-COMPASSION

Self-compassion, put simply, is about being kind to ourselves and resisting the urge to judge. Treating our mental health with a gentle touch is not so very hard once we begin to practise relaxing our grip, little by little; the irony is that we may actually achieve more by doing so.

THE TERM 'self-compassion' has become increasingly embraced by mindful musicians – indeed, some contemporary commentators believe it marks a milestone in the evolution of modern psychology. Self-compassion is by no means solely the province of the professional musician; the amateur regularly needs saving from himself, too. It's not so much about letting ourselves off the hook, but more about setting ourselves achievable goals. In practical terms, this might amount to acquainting ourselves with new music and paying closer heed to our current playing ability, or for the more senior musician, tackling repertoire that will not place undue strain on mental or physical resources. On the other hand, permitting ourselves to believe we will eventually be capable of achieving something that currently lies a little way out of reach is not a bad thing – the term 'fake it till you make it' springs to mind. Ideally, we need to feel challenged and excited, but never overwhelmed. Our mindset will often define our level of performance, in music just as in anything else; harnessed appropriately, stress can actually mobilize success and empower us. Excitement is in many ways the equivalent emotion to anxiety – we just need to frame it differently in our mind. Self-compassion means coming to an understanding with the stresses of life and choosing to be more rational about its causes. Self-compassion can help the conscientious listener, too. It might mean coming to terms with the fact that the music of a certain composer holds little value for us, leaving us free to explore other music with extra determination and listening energy.

The Australian pianist David Helfgott, whose fascinating life was controversially immortalized in the film *Shine*, suffers from schizoaffective disorder, the symptoms of which are groaning and displaying other bizarre mannerisms unwittingly, even when under the glare of a major public performance. Helfgott serves to remind us that a life-altering mental breakdown may be too high a price to pay for expecting too much of ourselves. There are no prizes for grinding ourselves into the dust; he who picks a fight with himself will surely end up losing, one way or another.

Compassion for Our World

Self-compassion leads logically to a compassion for our world, and this can take myriad artistic forms. The immediacy of music, and its capacity to draw from us ideas and emotions we could not even have imagined exist, accords it a similar status to poetry and art.

The global sensibility captured in a visionary soundscape might be described as a stream of consciousness – the white heat of emotion that a musician might channel in an act of supreme eloquence. Through the combined media of music and light, John Luther Adams came perhaps as close as any composer in modern times to capturing the essence of the apocalypse. Set against the backdrop of Alaska and the Pacific Northwest, *Become Ocean* is a twenty-minute orchestral spectacular in which three vast sections of music appear to be pitted against each other.

The French composer Olivier Messiaen composed his *Quartet for the End of Time* while incarcerated in occupied Poland during the Second World War. Not unlike Adams, Messiaen feared the world was slipping through all of our fingers, though his concerns possibly seemed even more imminent: Nazi world domination. Had it not been for the small but appreciable acts of generosity shown to him by one of the guards, Messiaen would never have been able to scribble down all those angst-ridden notes, let alone assemble four instruments barely fit for the purpose. It is impossible for us to imagine the abominable setting for the *Quartet*'s inaugural performance, given in torrential rain to nearly 500 soul-starved prisoners. If Messiaen's masterpiece does not constitute an act of supreme mindfulness through the medium of music, I do not know what does.

Mindfulness in music can be a timely metaphor for the conflicting ambitions we project onto our world. Perhaps we need to experience personal tragedy, incarceration or an unexpectedly profound insight before we can truly say we have something to be mindful about. On the other hand, we all live in the world of our heads, and the music that becomes potent in our lives helps us to connect our thoughts to our deeds. Perhaps this is why musicians such as Sting, in 'Russians', or the Sex Pistols with 'God Save the Queen', feel driven to comment on the world through their music. Their messages might not necessarily be ones we feel an affinity with, yet we can usually still relate to their soulful, occasionally rebuking mode of communication. Something similar happens every time a singer covers a song by Joan Baez, or a guitarist manages to unpick the iconic opening sequence to Led Zeppelin's 'Stairway to Heaven'.

Breathe, Breathe in the Air

Humans are hardwired to breathe, even when we sleep. But breathing provides more than just basic brain fuel – it injects buoyancy into our creative thinking and hence becomes the means by which we can achieve epic leaps of faith.

Remembering to breathe sounds utterly preposterous. And yet it seems we often forget to do this – ironically, just when our brains most need to be at their sharpest. Musicians from all walks of life seem prone to holding their breath when playing, which saps creativity and substitutes it with tension. I was once given a one-to-one juggling lesson with an American professional stage juggler called John Nations. I learned a great deal about coordination, concentration, the centre of gravity, my own clumsiness, and how long it had been since I challenged my brain (and body) with something entirely new. A mantra of his was 'Breathe, damn it!', prompted by my repeated failure to make a flow state remotely possible. He brushed off the evident tension in my arms and shoulders as the predictable, self-defeating trait of a rookie juggler, yet try as I might, keeping my breathing steady and regular seemed the hardest part of all. Things improved very slightly once he'd given me permission to drop the balls. 'All jugglers drop stuff,' he quipped stoically, 'we just pick it all up again and hope nobody noticed.' Breathing smoothly and rhythmically is within our control and is most certainly key to achieving success in so many things in life. Proficient musicians, irrespective of genre, instinctively know this to be the case, and yet it is not just wind players and singers who have to practise their breathing every day.

We all breathe in and out about 15–30 thousand times per day, so you might think that we are all born experts at breathing calmly and deeply – couch potatoes especially so. But this complacency is at the root of many problems, for before something can become absorbed into daily practice, we will almost invariably need to *practise* it. By this I mean that first we must grasp the essence of what we are attempting to do conceptually, then patiently acquire whatever mental or physical skills are needed, one by one. Breathing efficiently is how we connect body, mind and soul.

Mindfulness & Stillness

Some years ago I had the privilege of spending a morning in the company of a lama, sitting cross-legged at his humble place of residence about fifty miles from base camp at the foothills of Everest. The meeting left quite an impression on me, so much so that I subsequently composed 'Himalayan Suite' for flute and piano to commemorate my two months working in and around Northern India. The lama, a young man whose parents had single-handedly raised the funds to educate an entire micro-community, spoke a great deal about mindfulness and breathing. The potential for us all to bring about a state of emptiness, or stillness, was a subject he returned to time and again; he convinced me that mindful breathing can help us to achieve this, but only if we value it sufficiently to practise it.

Breathing smoothly and rhythmically is within our control and is most certainly key to achieving success in so many things in life

As a music educator, it seems clear to me that properly regulated breathing is central to success.

COUNTING OUT, ZONING IN

It may be interesting to know approximately what impact regulating our breathing can have. Start by sitting somewhere peaceful, preferably alone, and quickly take your approximate heart rate by counting your pulse over a period of ten seconds and multiplying by six. Assuming you are in good health, and you've not just emerged from having a sauna or running from a rabid dog, your heart rate could be, say, 70–90 bpm at rest. Now close your eyes and try to breathe very slowly, using long, regular motions. Take especial care to count up to ten and out to fifteen each time. I find it helpful to imagine my brain breathing too, not just my lungs. As you continue to do this for a couple of minutes, gradually focus your attention on your hearing. Absolute silence is among the rarest of commodities, so it is likely there will be at least some distant sound for you to lock on to. Acknowledge these sounds as they come to you, allow them to fade in and out, and simply continue to sit serenely.

Now take another pulse reading to see if you have managed to reduce your heart rate by a modest amount. After I'd been doing this for a month or so, I found I could slow my heart rate down by several bpm. Next time around, take an extended piece of ambient music – why not try Arvo Pärt's *Passio*, music that for me hangs in the air like a giant cobweb – and use this as a source for your meditation. In my own (admittedly somewhat unscientific) attempts, an appropriate musical impetus worked at least as well as none. Make time in your day to do this – it only takes as long as brewing a cup of coffee, but arguably will energize you more. If you are a practising musician, try this before rehearsing (or even midway through an extended session); you could also use it to steady yourself before you have a lesson.

Arguably we are all at our most defenceless and vulnerable when we lay ourselves bare before others, especially when the outcome of our efforts is something we care deeply about. It is impossible to play or sing music to the best of your ability when your heart is racing ten to the dozen, so it is a good idea to practise mindful breathing, and then visualize yourself in a more stressful environment to see what changes in your body and mind you can make by this simplest of exercises.

In the midst of a frenetic day of examining or teaching, I have trained myself to switch back and forth between two very different modes of thought: applying my critical faculties – that is, assessing, weighing up, pinpointing the various qualities that strike me – and simply *enjoying, experiencing*. There is a time and place for each, and for professional musicians especially it is important to transition from one mode to the other decisively.

In a nutshell, mindfulness in music is about nodding approvingly at sounds as they appear on our radar, rather than becoming locked in an exhausting mental debate. Music is part of our shared heritage, but not all music is capable of all things. Nevertheless, the music we find particularly conducive to mindfulness will help us to achieve that most magical of sensations: a mind and body in natural resonance with each other.

CHAPTER TWO

THE RHYTHM OF LIFE

We cannot feel the earth moving us along at a giddying thousand miles per hour, for even as we sleep we are moving with it at precisely the same speed. And yet the minute we wake up, our pace of life often feels even faster. But the pace of life and the pulse of our existence are two quite different things. Perhaps music holds the secret to life's rhythm. Music beats in time with our mood and can steer our day back on course in a single heartbeat.

The Ocean's Heartbeat

The ebb and flow of an ocean presents an irresistible parallel with the tide and time of our lives; a rhythm not tapped out in beats, but nonetheless dependable, dance-like and life sustaining. Feel its pulse quicken and chasten in step with yours.

Breathing calmly and flowingly can actually give us the impression of time slowing down. When we lock into every passing second, we appear able to stretch time, which is why a two-minute silent vigil can appear to take an eternity. Hence, for me, the perception of time has always been more a function of sound than sight – an ability to lock into each second as it melts away seems somehow more real when experienced primarily via the ears. Music happens in real time – often it has been carved up into manageable 'ticking' increments for us – and yet there are moments when time is buried so deeply into the music's core, our experience of it is altogether different. The human ear does not necessarily need a high level of organization or regularity in order to sense the passage of time: the sea's perpetual roar conveys it to us through motion alone.

When we consider how much mayhem is going on beneath the surface of the oceans – big fish chasing smaller ones, shoals of tightly choreographed mackerel darting at high speed, bull sharks and other predators vigilantly marking out their territories – we might imagine it to be teeming with sound. It is, but we never get to hear any of it – unless we are actually down there among the noisier creatures, such as whales, which can create sounds audible for hundreds of miles. We could almost think of these watery noises as akin to human organs, working away to keep us alive, and yet most of the time eerily silent to us. The ultrasounds emitted by dolphins – clicks and extreme high-frequency noises – are but one small measure of the cacophony playing itself out below the surface. All of the marine sound that is happening gets bounced back down towards the seabed, just as the sound we hear above sea level gets reflected skywards; never the twain shall meet. Whereas light tends to be more important for us above sea level, enabling us to see far into the distance, sound becomes the more important currency below sea level – increasingly so as we plummet deeper and deeper, until the light eventually drains away to virtually nothing.

Ambient Music

The sound of the humpback whale is often considered particularly relaxing for humans. One reason could be the slow onset and decay of such sounds (rainforests and waterfalls likewise), in stark contrast with sharp, more abrupt noises – even ones that might seem relatively quiet, such as a human whisper. Unannounced, edgy sounds of any sort jar in our ears and will generally trigger the emotion of fear or trepidation, while steady, progressive sounds are often deemed to be soothing, soporific even. The genre of ambient music easily dismissed as 'spa' is effective precisely because it meanders and avoids drawing attention to itself.

Like an exotic aroma, ambient music lingers for just long enough to permeate our consciousness, then drifts away again. By no means all music is equally self-effacing; exercising mindfulness can easily appear at odds with music's determination to win over our imagination. It is for each of us to gauge the point at which music, or natural sound for that matter, seeks too much of our attention and hence becomes counterproductive.

LISTEN TO BIOMUSIC

Biomusic is music that either mimics, replicates or electronically distorts the sounds produced by non-humans. In many cases, such music will make daring use of the sounds produced by plants or animals, usually amplified and manipulated to create an appealing, perhaps ethereal effect. New-Age music might be considered a subgenre of biomusic; it combines these kinds of effects with real or digital instruments, often with an amount of post-production or reverb to further merge reality with unreality. A work of significance that falls into this latter category is *And God Created Great Whales*, composed by the American composer Alan Hovhaness in 1970. The music successfully integrates the songs of the humpback, bowhead and killer whales with an orchestra – a truly sublime piece.

Music & Movement

An ability to move with music – physically move – may be as important as having the capacity to be moved by music. Rhythm isn't there to keep music tightly corseted – quite the opposite; it is something our bodies find irresistibly impulsive.

Importantly, a considerable amount of music, from any genre, is recognizable by its rhythm alone. Perhaps, when you were younger, you were encouraged to dance and move easily with certain types of music? This kind of activity seems to have become less in vogue these days, except perhaps among the more enlightened music-and-movement group lessons in kindergarten/prep schools. In my teaching, I often encourage students to move freely around the room – I also find myself moving to their playing; this is usually a good sign, actually, as it demonstrates to the student that their playing has begun to acquire better momentum and direction. Movement is not just for those learning to dance (or indeed play), it is intrinsic to music itself – not all music, of course, but a surprising amount of it. What better lesson in playing waltzes or tangos can there be than dancing around the room in time to the music?

Free movement is something that might take some getting used to, either as part of a group or even on your own. Responding rhythmically to music while jogging or working out in the gym is commonplace enough, and yet these are both

'We should consider every day lost on which we have not danced at least once.'

Friedrich Nietzsche (1844–1900)
German philosopher

high-energy activities intended to help us to fire on all cylinders, not to rejoice in the movement captured in the music itself, however slow and contemplative it might be. A *pas de deux* in our heads can be as lithe and elegant as any ballet dancer – but we might still allow ourselves to physically move.

Qigong & Tai Chi

When walking in the morning heat to catch the train in Hong Kong and Singapore, I have been frequently reminded of the power of music and movement. Qigong ('life energy cultivation') is a form of Chinese exercise, or 'moving meditation', with its roots in the martial arts, which continues to play an important part in many people's daily lives, not just in China but all over the Far East and beyond. Qigong already plays a valuable role for some more liberally minded music teachers in the West, too, such as the British pianist and teacher Andrew Eales, whose website pianodao.com is certainly worth more than a passing glance. There are many other highly beneficial forms of movement, such as the circular slow motion characteristic of tai chi, practised by millions of people in America and Europe, not just Asia, and which holds terrific potential to improve physical and mental well-being. These movement-based activities, especially when combined with music, succeed where so many of the 'frozen' approaches to learning *about* music may appear to be falling short in the West. Music can also be of enormous value when used in conjunction with yoga and Pilates – indeed, by tapping into the combined functions of physical movement, music and mindfulness, a whole spectrum of exciting possibilities opens itself up for us.

Alexander Technique

It is probably realistic to expect some amount of collateral damage as we pursue our hobbies and our sporting or musical endeavours. Few of us stop to question how we bend down to pick something up, for instance, or how we stand up again, let alone those aspects of more complex coordinated movement that enable us to drive a car, or play a bassoon. Our unquestioning assumption – that our bodies are already functioning optimally – may well be holding us back. Frederick Alexander, a Shakespeare orator born in 1869, self-diagnosed his persistent problems of speech loss by surrounding himself with mirrors, monitoring and adjusting his movements according to what his eyes taught him. By such means he was able to detect the various involuntary motions of his head and neck that were effectively foreshortening his stature and restricting his airflow just prior to orating. These contortions, he quickly realized, were potentially the root cause of similar debilitating symptoms experienced by others, not just in his own field but in a wide range of others. Alexander would later set out his ground-breaking discoveries in the form of four books, published between 1918 and 1942. In essence, his teachings sought to address problems associated with ungainly posture, unnatural muscular movements and unbalanced weight distribution, the sum of which can lead to all manner of undesirable manifestations of tension. Alexander's findings opened up other fruitful avenues of thought, too – for example, how gravity might be more gainfully harnessed to assist with uninhibited movement.

Alexander Technique does not stop there; it is also about teaching us to harmonize freer bodies with freer minds, and ultimately to become more patient with ourselves. Although the potential connections between Alexander's awareness of 'self' – and mindfulness – might seem abundantly clear to us today, Alexander did not actually employ the term mindfulness, though his books contain a great deal of which the mindful contemporary musician and non-musician might do well to be aware. Perhaps the most important thing to bear in mind is that the responsibility to begin the fixing process is ours. Thankfully, Alexander teachers are experts at observing others – and being observed themselves. Unlike many music teachers, myself included, Alexander teachers are reliably able to demonstrate best practice, though the approach must always be student-centric because we all exhibit subtly different body geometry.

There is, therefore, no single approach or strategy by which success can be achieved. Learning Alexander Technique, not unlike practising mindfulness, is not something we can pick up in a few minutes, but needs to be thought about and embraced as an overarching philosophy.

Are You Sitting Comfortably?

When we stop to think of it, the design of very few musical instruments can be considered conducive to a body in harmony with itself. Singers continually need to be shown how to optimize their flow state, for their body *is* of course also their instrument. Most of us learn to compensate for such built-in challenges by unwittingly realigning our 'body technology', but the truth is we place ourselves in harm's way the day we take up a guitar, accordion or penny whistle unless we go about it thoughtfully. Arguably, a harpist is at least able to place her arms with the hands facing in towards each other, as they naturally gravitate to being, unlike a pianist, who has to turn them ninety degrees outwards to even contemplate striking a note.

Exaggerated and compensatory movements can find their way into a musician's actions without them even being aware they are there. Repetitive strain injury or RSI – for warehouse workers and sports enthusiasts as much as musicians – is generally considered to be at least partly attributable to poor posture, as is tension in general, and those who play most musical instruments seem prone to encountering problems somewhere along the line unless they take care of such things from a younger age. Just think how non-ergonomic sitting astride a cello is, for instance, or leaning over a double bass in order to reach the high notes, let alone the sizeable weight-bearing done by trombone or baritone saxophone players, even if they choose to sit when they play. Flute players might have a fraction of the metalwork to grapple with compared with tuba players, but they must still deport themselves optimally, else the weight of their own limbs can be great enough to do considerable damage over the longer term. Unless we take care to work *with* ourselves, we will forever be in opposition with ourselves.

Music Appreciation

Audiences at classical concerts and recitals have a tendency to appear outwardly uninvolved (a notable exception being 'The Last Night of the Proms', in London's Royal Albert Hall). Indeed, such occasions often more closely resemble lectures (or funerals even) than joyful musical celebrations. This seems paradoxical, particularly since Renaissance and baroque composers were often preoccupied with lively dance forms. We should probably assume collective responsibility for this puzzling level of introspection, for we appear to have unaccountably lost our capacity to move uninhibitedly. After all, larger classical works such as sonatas, concertos and symphonies are almost invariably partitioned off into 'movements', which to me implies a sense of journeying – moving – through the music's various moods.

The assumption that classical music is best served up cold is decidedly not true of most other forms of music that have evolved during the past hundred years or so. Pop, rock, jazz and folk-fusion audiences expect there to be a far less constrained kinship between what is happening in one's head and what is happening with one's body. The idea of sitting motionless at a U2 concert seems utterly ridiculous – we would be missing the point of the occasion entirely. Importantly, we can hardly discuss the possibility of physical movement in a live music setting without accepting some level of collateral noise. What counts as a respectful restraint for a classical guitar recital would seem anathema to audiences attending a jazz gig, where foot-tapping and moving in time with the music is not merely considered acceptable, it is entirely factored into the experience.

On my second tour to India and Bangladesh, I gave a lecture-recital to 1,200 people. On reflection, I imagine the audience was probably a little trepidatious about what they were to hear. I was, too – I'd been told to expect a dozen people. To my amazement, and joy, spontaneous applause erupted while I was actually playing; en masse, the audience showed their appreciation of particular passages by rising to their feet and clapping ecstatically, then sitting back down again, in as unconstrained a way as I have ever personally experienced. Not for a moment did I feel the behaviour rude or disrespectful.

Music & Sleep

Meditation achieves much that sleep promises; we re-emerge vivid and sentient. Tonight, as we sleep, perhaps we will discover ourselves washed up on the shore of some long-forgotten dream, with the vestiges of a far-off melody licking up around our ankles.

Depictions of music aiding sleep go back to the time of the ancient Greeks, but we receive conflicting advice these days regarding the potential for outside forces to assist us when we are struggling to nod off. For example, some sleep specialists appear convinced that substituting your regular light bulb for a red one will do the trick, due to its positive impact on the body's melatonin levels. Others caution against any kind of so-called 'light pollution' because it might invoke negative mood swings that could even lead to depression and a variety of alarming physical ailments.

It can be strangely illuminating to wander around for a few days wearing your dressing gown like Noel Coward in a semi-somnolent state; some of my most inspirational thoughts seem to occur in a trance. Assuming there are no underlying medical issues to exacerbate your erratic sleeping, music and mindfulness are valuable tools you can use to nudge the odds further in your favour. You could try one of a growing number of apps, which range from providing customizable ambient sounds such as rain, whales or birdsong to those that offer a more sophisticated solution whereby your device analyses your sleep pattern and then gently coaxes you awake at a point when you are not too deeply asleep.

Other home-grown solutions also await your attention, and this is where a little self-knowledge is invaluable. As a student, I spent a couple of months working at an American summer camp in the Catskill Mountains, New York State, where the norm was for loud rock music to blare out throughout the day and night in the communal bunkhouse. Initially, it drove me crazy and made me resentful of my persistently interrupted sleep – worse still, if I dared to turn it off, there was an immediate uprising. Weirdly, bit by bit I succumbed to the soporific effect of Run-DMC and Bruce Springsteen; I think it was when I gave myself permission to bow to the inevitable, stop judging the music and expect to have it booming away that matters improved. I was reminded of this bizarre experience recently when I heard about a man who was initially kept awake by a noisy light bulb for many years (he worked in a submarine, if I recall correctly), but eventually became so used to it he found he later had to mimic its effect in order to get to sleep.

'Music that gentlier on the spirit lies,
Than tir'd eyelids upon tir'd eyes'

From 'Song of the Lotos-Eaters'
Alfred, Lord Tennyson (1809–1892), British poet

Mindful & Musical Tips to Assist with Sleep

1. Do some mindful breathing shortly before you retire. This will slow down your body and mind and prepare you for sleep.

2. Experiment with a variety of sound sources, and be aware that certain musical instruments, such as the flute, accordion and guitar, may prove more conducive to sleep than others.

3. Initially, try slow, repetitive music that meanders, or appears 'static', rather than music that seems busy or continually to be driven towards high points. It could be classical, biomusic, rock ballads, ambient or electronic – but anything is valid if it works for you.

4. Be aware that if you wake up, the music needs to be sufficiently unobtrusive to corral you gently back to the land of Nod.

5. Try blending earth sounds, either from apps or that you have recorded for yourself, along with your chosen music. Blending the optimum cocktail of sounds could be your ticket to dreamland.

6. Aim, if at all feasible, to make the final hour or two of your day a time of quiet repose. Mentally battening down the hatches is important; avoid fatiguing or overly stimulating challenges such as sudoku puzzles, turn off the TV, and maybe read a page or two of something easy-going as you tune in to your chosen soundscape.

7. Aided by your chosen sounds, instruct each part of your body to go to sleep, one by one: first one foot, then the other, etc.

8. Imagine each limb to be ten times its usual weight, bearing downwards through to the floor below.

Living the Dream

When I sleep, music invariably permeates my dreams. Strange how my spontaneous backing tracks subtly mould the way each dream wants to unfold. Some strands of music end up taking on intriguing life forms of their own. Though I can rarely fathom whether my dreams actually mean anything, I can usually replay vestiges of the music well into the morning. People are sometimes encouraged to jot down their dreams, but it occurs to me there may be as much to be learned from trying to reimagine the sounds, or perhaps music, that helped to make them so vivid. Next time you find yourself recounting a bizarre dream to a friend, tell them about the music. Music's other-worldliness may be its most powerful, compelling facet.

Music as Stimulation

Whether certain forms of music demonstrate quantifiable, enduring qualities of enhancement, as measured by IQ, spatial intelligence or other cognitive yardsticks, remains controversial. All that matters, surely, is what ignites *us*. Were it to turn out that more people in the West are stimulated by, say, Mozart's music than hip hop or psychedelic funk, this might not be altogether surprising – though I suspect myriad cultural, experiential and generational biases would influence such a finding. In music, beauty is always in the ear of the beholder.

CHAPTER THREE

SOUND & SENSUALITY

How can we be interested in the sound of nature if we are not intrigued by the nature of sound? Regardless of whether we have the capacity to fathom what it might be, every sound is there to serve its own particular purpose and hence reveals a great deal about itself, if only we care to notice. Noticing is indeed a fundamental quality of mindfulness; when we are observant to sound, it repays us by revealing even more of itself.

The Sound of Life Itself

Being alive to natural sound starts with heightening our level of awareness: expecting beauty, yet still delighting in its discovery. From here we become better tuned in to our environment, and at the same time more in resonance with the music we know and love.

When we think how spectacular the sounds are that we are able to hear, we should probably pause for a moment to marvel at those we cannot. Hold a stethoscope to a tree on a warm day and you might be surprised that it is not silent but faintly crackling, as its roots suck up moisture from the ground and create microscopic bubbles that are forming close to its bark. We might not be able to *see* sound as such, but we can certainly see what effect it is having all around us: place a loudspeaker next to a naked flame and watch it dance to the tune that is playing; or play a loud note on your trombone up close to a thin pane of glass and watch it shudder as if with excitement. A murmuration of starlings is as much about sound in motion as motion in

'One's ideas must be as broad as Nature
if they are to interpret Nature.'

from *A Study in Scarlet*
Arthur Conan Doyle (1859–1930), British writer

sound. For me, these unannounced, 'telepathically' coordinated swirling gestures resemble a Mahler symphony, forever rolling forwards and reshaping itself.

The relationship between an object and the sound it makes therefore renders it a little like a fingerprint – unique and special to itself. For this reason, your voice will be different from mine in far more obvious ways acoustically than we could ever hope to reveal using laryngoscopy. So when we hear an object or creature make a sound, we are really getting a rich spectrum of frequencies that accumulate, not the single source we imagine triggered it. We all know that a skilled player will be able to make a relatively pleasing sound, even on a poor-quality musical instrument. And yet, even with the aid of an MRI scan, the subtle difference between a seasoned player and a novice might not be so easy to detect when they play; after all, when it comes to creating music, we are dealing with a dizzying array of permutations, and at least as many possible perceptions.

The origin of a sound, though an indispensable trigger for any musical instrument or voice, is but one of its key components. From its source, it then requires amplification – a resonator – which can project the sound out into a space far greater than seems realistic when we consider the tiny metallic surface of, say, a harmonica or a triangle. The more sophisticated and adaptable the resonator, the more flexible and wonderful the sounds it will potentially be capable of making. This is where the human being steps into the equation, for when it comes to singing especially, all these physical attributes require the subtlest of handling. Singers do not need a degree in physics or physiognomy, and yet by harnessing their raw instrument in concert with individual characteristics of hearing, something rather special happens. Accomplished musicians are also acousticians, able to monitor and modify the sound they are producing moment by moment, thereby producing an effect that (thankfully) can never be replicated or equalled by technology.

For Whom the Bell Tolls

If we love the sound of our village church bell, it is probably because its natural frequencies were calculated hundreds of years earlier specifically to produce several 'notes' simultaneously in something close to a harmonious ratio with each other; a bell does not produce the random wash of sound we might imagine it to. Bells, unlike most other man-made sound creators (technically, bells come under the category of tuned

'For bells are the voice of the church;
They have tones that touch and search
The hearts of young and old.'

From 'The Bells of San Blas'
Henry Wadsworth Longfellow (1807–82), American poet

CHIME, CHIME, CHIME

The meditative quality of bells is palpable, whether you happen to be a ringer or listening from afar. As you listen, see how many notes you can pick out from each bell – sing them out loud, or in your head; this is a way of bonding even more closely with it. A ring of bells may be even more conducive to meditation – or better still, a peal, which might involve 5,000 so-called 'changes'. A friend of mine enjoys collecting random sounds, such as bells, on his recording device, rather as most of us do unthinkingly with our phone's on-board camera. This is a lovely way of storing away our travel memories for future reflection.

percussion instruments), do not go out of tune, even those that came from what many regard as the heyday of bell-making in southern Europe, the seventeenth century. Had a bell been founded slightly thinner, larger or from a different metal, the sound it so proudly emits would be wholly different. If we listen closely to a single bell, we may be able to detect several separate notes stacked upon each other in countable steps, or 'partials', of three, four or eight – straight away we have the basis for a symphony here, for the term literally means 'sounding together'. Though the nominal partial of a church bell might be, say, an E (an example being Big Ben in London), most of us will actually perceive the A to be its dominant harmonic, four notes higher.

Due to the inevitable imprecisions brought about by human timing and ancient architecture, it is comparatively rare to hear what a musician would call 'rhythmic' bell-ringing, even if the correct pattern for each 'row' was followed. For bell-ringers (campanologists), it would seem that algorithm is more important than rhythm. Nonetheless, we can derive musical meaning and meditative potential from the sound of a bell, especially if we try to hear the beginning, middle and end of each and every strike.

Filter Out the 'Other' Stuff

The word 'sound' can be slightly misleading when it crops up in everyday parlance, for rarely will it be the case that we are presented with just one pure sound, whether in a musical or non-musical sense. I am not referring to so-called 'white noise', which turns out to have a variety of possible connotations, but to ordinary, everyday sounds. Take, for example, the rumpus of a busy cafe. If we listen intently, we may notice the sound equivalent to a 'layered' landscape painting – foreground, middle-ground and background – with perhaps subtler shades in between. In the background there will probably be an indistinguishable murmur of voices; in the middle-ground we become aware of intermittent espresso machines; and in the foreground there are the voices of several friends, laughing and interrupting each other. In brief patches, a few notes of mood music percolate through

LISTEN TO THE CALL OF THE MUEZZIN

Ever since minarets have been built adjacent to mosques in Muslim countries, the amplified voice of the muezzin – whose job it is to recite the Muslim call to prayer (Ezan) – has given something memorable and special to casual visitors, although its function is of course to summon worshippers five times per day, not to provide periodic entertainment for non-Muslim visitors. When you visit a Muslim country such as Turkey, it is a real privilege to hear the Ezan, even if at first the sleep disruption at dawn may be a little disconcerting! In fact, the skill of chanting the Ezan is taken so seriously in Turkey that there is a competition between muezzins.

Three things particularly worth noticing are the elaborate chants themselves, always highly individual (though some are prerecorded), meditative and lyrical; the sheer length of each chant, which would certainly test the breath control of a Western trained singer; and the mesmerizing overlap of simultaneous Ezans as they emanate from nearby mosques, accumulating into some ear-boggling harmonies that you can feel free to use as a trigger for your own meditation. For me, listening to Ezans, or indeed the wonderfully soulful clarinettists improvising on the streets of Istanbul, Izmir and Ankara, reminds me that music – just as with mindfulness – is always of its moment. In the next moment, it is gone again, leaving space for something else just as intoxicating.

to provide a softer ambience. A door suddenly opens, or a mobile phone detonates into life across the way – these are, if you like, the soundscape equivalents to the seagulls painted onto an artist's landscape; afterthoughts almost, and yet vital to a sense of perspective and realism.

Welcome to My Office

On a visit to Tahiti, our wonderfully able guide, Teuai, drove us along a narrowing dirt track deep into Fautaua Valley. It has thirty impressive waterfalls, which bring what he optimistically described as an endless supply of water to keep the surrounding mountains lush. Teuai brought the jeep to a halt, turned to us and smiled, 'Welcome to my office.' He then retrieved a conch and showed us how his ancestors had used the shell for communication in centuries past – each guttural, penetrating tone issued forth into the valley for perhaps eight seconds. He then demonstrated how members of his tribe would have signalled their arrival at another part of the island by striking the base of a tree trunk with a heavy rock. Different rhythms would have had a variety of meanings, the simplest consisting of three bold strikes of increasingly higher pitch, formed by aiming slightly higher up the trunk at each strike. 'Heavy rock music,' he grinned, 'but not Motörhead.'

For Teuai's ancestors the sounds made with both the tree and the shell were emblematic of three potent elements all wrapped into one: man working in harmony with the land, the music of the forest and the need to communicate from one corner of the valley to another. It all made satisfying sense as we stood there, panting from the heat. As if from nowhere, Teuai calmly produced his iPhone and called his mother – from Fautaua Valley to Silicon Valley in the blink of an eye, an odd conclusion to a memorable tour.

Because our ears instantly attune to each new sound as it fades in and out of focus, we may mistake it for a meaningless jumble. But if we take a moment to peel away at it, our sound-environments nearly always transcend cacophony and take on an individual beauty. Indeed, dissonance – both in music and in life – often proves to be more interesting than consonance. It is not that our ears cannot cope with this complex melange of sounds, just that we often do not bother to filter them through. In music, every single note played on, say, a piano or clarinet consists of many complex overtones; it is the aural alchemy of these that gives each its characteristic tone, or timbre. Learning to listen more acutely is not about being 'disciplined' as such, but aiming to filter out those elements that at that particular moment appear less interesting to us. A good place to start is the caffeine-infused maelstrom that is whipping up all around you in your local coffee shop; from here, you can revisit your favourite progressive rock track, modern jazz piece or symphony with sharper ears. Zoom in on each layer of sound, one by one – say, bass, drums and vocals – then follow it along as though none of the others was happening; finally, zoom back out to get the full effect. This is what skilled sound engineers do every day – aided, of course, by faders on their mixing desk.

The Colour of Music

Musicians and listeners are often given to attributing colour to sound, or indeed sound to colour. Though the origin of this fascination is not clear, the attractiveness of a parallel between hues or shades of 'real' colour and their possible equivalents in sound is for many musicians irresistible.

Perhaps an artist's palette is not so far removed from a musician's tonal 'swatch' – for in each case it will be the nuanced details and the possibility for adding subtle personal touches that will probably seem most attractive. Just as in art, where shadows, reflections or other oblique references to a light source are invaluable, in music also much can be made of the power of suggestion – the faintest allusion to something slightly out of place, or indeed an unsettling hint of 'darkness'. It is not uncommon for musicians to associate keys with particular 'personalities' too, although in practice these tend to be highly idiosyncratic, not something holding universal currency. For example, the 'bright' key of C major would probably be suggestive of a rather different colour from the contrastingly 'warm' key of D flat major, just a half-step higher. In such cases there can be an amusing degree of disagreement among musicians, although it is certainly true that much mellifluous, dreamy piano music is composed in keys containing lots of flats.

And then there is the more literal sense in which colour becomes automatically and involuntarily mapped onto sound – or, of course, the other way around. 'Synaesthesia' is the term used to describe a person's internalized response to sound in this way, though it can also apply to other equally intriguing pathway connections, for example colour and taste. The disorder known as misophonia, for example, is a variant in which a strong negative reaction to a particular sound arises – perhaps rejection or repulsion. Synaesthetes, in their many different permutations, make up about 4 per cent of the population; my own synaesthesia is among the more common forms and has, for as long as I can remember, been more or less restricted to an association between colours and days of the week (for me, Tuesday is burgundy). Associations of this type have been known to help people perform extraordinary feats of recall, though it is important to understand that one does not manufacture synaesthesia in one's own mind, nor is it usually considered in any way a handicap.

'Colour and sound are not only the language in which
one communicates with the life without,
but also the language in which one communicates
with the life within.'

FROM *THE MYSTICISM OF SOUND AND MUSIC*
HAZRAT INAYAT KHAN (1882–1927)
INDIAN MUSICIAN AND FOUNDER OF THE SUFI ORDER IN THE WEST

It is interesting to see what synaesthetes can achieve creatively, although the overlap between synaesthesia and a somewhat looser, more instinctive sense of a connection between certain sensory pathways will not always be easy to ascertain. The Russian composer Alexander Scriabin was not a synaesthete, despite the strong colour contrivances revealed in much of his music. Olivier Messiaen was, however, known to have been highly influenced by his synaesthesia – also musicians Billy Joel and Mickey Hart of the band The Grateful Dead. Artists similarly influenced include David Hockney and Wassily Kandinsky. In music, the outcome is often vastly different among synaesthetes, although they can generally be seen to draw from an unusually rich bank of tonal colours.

TAKE A MAGICAL MUSICAL MYSTERY TOUR

Your choice of music may well mirror your mood at any particular moment in time. The mesmerizing mix of musical tastes that we carry around with us will probably feel 'logical' in the sense that we immediately recognize ourself as the owner. It's a bit like your choice of colour scheme in your home, which is probably not as random as you imagine – 'cool' colours for the bathroom perhaps, and 'warmer' ones for the living room. Actually, the more random your musical preferences appear to be, the more interesting and revealing they will be to other people. If you'd like to take a glimpse at what it might be like to live in sometime else's skin, why not swap playlists for a weekend?

Their complex harmonies seem governed by extreme – at times almost violent – variety. If visionaries are able to see things differently, it follows that some musicians will hear things differently.

Why Elephants Listen with Their Feet

We tend to assume that listening is a response to sound that involves the ears in complete isolation. But listening means 'to give attention in order to hear' and, intriguingly, elephants – and some humans too – seem able to pick up meaningful resonances through their limbs.

It seems logical that quality of hearing will be, at least in part, a function of ear size. If this assumption has any validity, elephants surely come out way on top, African elephants having ears roughly the size of a double bed, about three times the size of their Indian counterparts. On the other hand, the greater wax moth (smaller than a matchbox) outstrips a human's hearing by 150 times. Bigger ears mean cooler bodies, which is handy if you happen to inhabit the Maasai Mara, though it is certainly easier to measure the physical proportions of an animal's ears than to assess its hearing capacities – let alone its *listening* capacities. Indeed, many of the cognitive tests we might perform on humans will not necessarily be appropriate for an animal. However, it seems likely that the African elephant is able to detect a fellow animal's foot-thumping from as far off as 150 miles, or helicopters approaching from 100 miles away; it probably achieves this by a combination of acute hearing and an ability to pick up seismic low frequencies through nerve endings in its feet. What seems most intriguing, apart from the physical attributes that permit such perception (elephants can hear 20 Hz lower than humans), is the meaning these animals potentially glean from doing so. There is anecdotal evidence to suggest that elephants can detect the differences between African tribal languages, distinguish between men's and women's voices, and may even derive pleasure from listening to music.

Good Vibrations

It is conceivable, however, that by studying animals in such ways we run the risk of mapping human characteristics onto them. But remarkable these animals most certainly are, and it is with especial regard to the connection between an elephant's hearing and its listening that we can possibly learn a little about ourselves. Humans can, to varying degrees, pick up meaningful vibrations, too. The Scottish percussionist Dame Evelyn Glennie has a staggering capacity to function as a top soloist while possessing virtually no hearing (it had substantially disappeared by the age of 12). By perceiving both pitch and rhythm through vibration alone, these vibrations are detected through much of her body, not just her hands. In contrast with Glennie, who quickly rejected hearing aids, Beethoven reportedly went to great lengths to counter his impending deafness, trying a variety of ear trumpets and even attempting to pick up resonances from his keyboard by placing one end of a pencil in his mouth and touching the soundboard with the other.

IT TAKES TWO TO TANGO

Don't miss out on chances to be creative with sound in your day-to-day life. Though hardly 'natural', your electric toothbrush makes a remarkably stable and dependable duet partner. Mine happens to be pitched exactly on middle C, though it 'decays' a little when the battery starts to run down. Twice a day, I hum out loud to the accompaniment of my trusty toothbrush – sometimes I find myself strangely drawn to making a bagpipe drone effect whereby I hum five notes higher than the brush, or I might deliberately distort my pitching by bending the sound flatter or sharper than the brush, just to see if I can create 'nodes' – pulsating sound waves of the sort you get when piano strings are not tuned correctly.

Using the pitch produced by your electric toothbrush (or shaver) as a bass note, start and finish each day by humming or singing. Make up something on the spot that starts and finishes on the note given by the buzz, or else run through whichever melodies you happen to have floating around in your head at the time. You may even find other members of your household chiming in to make life-affirming chords.

Such is our endless quest for sound and sensuality. Thankfully, we never have far to hunt, or long to wait – for sound *is* life. I find it reassuring to remind myself that a surprisingly small amount of life exists in anything close to total silence. But it falls on us to seek out the sound of the natural world, otherwise it will all too quickly slip behind a tree, scamper into the long grass or hold its breath for just long enough to make us doubt it was ever there at all.

CHAPTER FOUR

THE LANGUAGE OF MUSIC

We all mean different things when we refer to the language of music. Whether or not music truly resembles a language, there can be no doubting its power to impart meaning. Besides, in mindfulness, 'literal' language is mostly rendered somewhat superfluous – after all, we are endeavouring to commune with ourselves, not to communicate with others. Far from being intrinsically selfish or inward looking, mindful activities encourage us to reflect, contemplate and help ourselves in so many practical ways. On balance, emotion appears to be the place where music, language and mindfulness come together most compellingly.

Ambiguity

When music speaks to us, words quickly seem superfluous. Music seeps into the nooks and crannies words leave unfilled, yet, intriguingly, its ambiguities still permit us to feel what we want to feel. Whatever deeper mysteries await our attention, music's poetic meaning always wins through.

It is often asserted that music is a universal language – or even the language of peace. Attractive though it may be, this view seems rather questionable when taken at face value. The word 'language', after all, implies a high level of precision and consistency by which information can be conveyed back and forth. Is this really what is taking place when we lose ourselves in, say, a Vangelis album, or find ourselves transfixed at a candle-lit midnight mass? If music has the properties of language, it follows that we should all be capable of perceiving a similar 'meaning' in a particular piece when we sit in our living rooms with the speakers cranked up high and a cat purring on our knee. And yet our individual receptivity to music surely

'What the music I love expresses to me are not thoughts too indefinite for words, but rather, too definite.'

Felix Mendelssohn (1809–1847)
German composer and pianist

You Say Goodbye and I Say Hello

I once taught piano to a bright Ukrainian boy whose English was equal to my Ukrainian: zero. By the end of one year I had learned to say 'hello' ('алло') and he'd learned to say 'goodbye' ('прощання'). More importantly, under my tutelage (but mostly due to considerable dedication on his part) he had learned, memorized and performed several significant pieces by his favourite composer, Rachmaninov. Lessons tended to follow a predictable pattern: he would play, I would point, we both would laugh, he would play again and I would nod. Enough said.

stems from its very subjectivity; far from being a shortcoming, music's open-endedness turns out to be its most precious facet. Music leaves all verbal and written communication standing – not because music is a language, but because it enables us to grasp what cannot be said with words alone.

A Minor Deviation

There is a long-established consensus that music in a minor key leans towards sounding melancholic or downbeat, while a sunnier, more upbeat mood frequently springs from music composed in a major key. But, as with so many other generalizations in music, inconvenient contradictions abound. The song 'Over the Rainbow', from *The Wizard of Oz*, is memorably contemplative yet cast in a major key, while Mozart's racy *Rondo alla Turca* and Supertramp's punchy 'Breakfast in America' were both composed in a minor key. This merely illustrates that for music to communicate something valuable it must first be filtered through the physical apparatus of our ears, and then allowed to negotiate the bubbling fountain of our imagination. Emotion in music, just as in real life in fact, is a moveable feast; it alters moment by moment.

When we hear something rather marvellous in a piece of music, or find ourselves strangely enchanted by the sound of someone speaking in a particular language for that matter, we learn something about ourselves, our perceptions and possibly even our prejudices. Hence, my personal feeling that the Italian language sounds more naturally melodious than some other European languages is surely based upon my own cultural values and baggage of experiences; there are no universal truths where sound perception is concerned, only ambiguities.

Music: Poetry in Motion

If the spoken word has the power to move us, music is poetry in motion. Take Toru Takemitsu's dream-inspired *A Flock Descends into the Pentagonal Garden*, the title of which quickly prepares the imagination for the composer's peculiarly aromatic soundworld. The music itself, however, contains no words at all. Paradoxically, what makes music an incomparable human experience is its resistance to being summed up in any amount of words. Even the most incisive wordsmith can never describe music adequately – only perhaps the experience of having heard it. The same applies to a title, no matter how alluring or descriptive.

Since time immemorial, songwriters have almost invariably relied upon a text, be it borrowed, improvised on the hoof or written specifically for the purpose, in order to help them convey a sharper emotional meaning in their songs. So-called 'word painting' has been a commonly employed tactic among composers through the ages to lend a song added poignancy; for example, the word 'high', used in conjunction with a sung high note, or the word 'softly' coupled with a hushed tone. Invariably, such highly specific connotations disappear behind frosted glass the moment we are deprived of hearing the words, which of course is what happens when songs are turned into instrumental arrangements.

Opera: Passion, Intrigue, Myth & Tragedy

Opera is one of the glistening pinnacles of music history; some would argue, of humanity itself. Its completeness as an art form, and its capacity to sum up the world in a nutshell, captivated the likes of Claudio Monteverdi in the early seventeenth century and, more recently, the Finnish composer Einojuhana Rautavaara, who died in 2016, attracting Mozart, Verdi, Puccini and Wagner along the way. Romantic opera is often a particularly emotional roller-coaster, yet paradoxically slow-burning and elaborate; composers usually seem grittily intent upon pointing us towards high points of emotional ecstasy. Chinese opera is older still, with its roots tracing back a thousand years; its mesmerizing combination of martial arts, music and theatre, dance, literature – even acrobatics – marks it out as a spectacle of human achievement.

Opera lovers often return to experience a favourite opera time and time again, curious as to how a different production or group of soloists will tackle it. They will probably have soaked up many of its ingenious twists and turns, just as others feast upon reruns of a particular movie or musical, or return to a much-admired book many times over. Opera finds its way into movies, adverts, jingles, ringtones and of course a whole gamut of genres: 'Barcelona', featuring Spanish soprano Montserrat Caballé in duet with Freddie Mercury, would be an obvious example.

For those of us who have to resort to reading an opera's subtitles, however, a great deal often seems to have evaporated into thin air even before it reaches us. Indeed, were we to airbrush out the libretto altogether (an opera's underlying text, or story), be it profound, passionate or tongue-in-cheek, its meaning would in most cases disappear behind a veiled curtain. Admittedly, some measure of the emotion and drama bound up in all the singing, orchestral music, costumes and stagecraft can still make for a memorably uplifting experience, even without mugging up on the plot or principal characters beforehand. But even if we feel we know a particular chorus or aria well by its melodic shape, its deeper meaning will not make itself known to us unless we happen to possess a fair grasp of the languages used most commonly in

GARAGE MUSIC

❋

Take one of your all-time favourite songs and sing it aloud to yourself in the garage, in the car, or perhaps in the park as you take your dog for its morning walk. Really think about the meaning behind each word, as though you were hearing it sung by someone else for the very first time. Now, as you sing it again, see if you can pinpoint a few specific things about the shape of the melody itself, i.e. particular high and low points, less usual intervals between notes, or places where the tune changes as its verses or choruses are repeated. Do any of these melodic features seem to fit particularly well with a certain word or group of words? Has the songwriter used word-painting anywhere to especially good effect? Finally, sing it through again, but to 'la', and ask yourself this: what, if anything, has been lost, and what in the song remains just as firmly in place?

The next time you find yourself singing or listening to the same song, you may well feel you know it even better. It's a little like reacquainting yourself with an old school friend whom you've not seen for years; you still know them for who they are, and yet differences in their physical appearance, personality and attitude to life bring a further dimension to your understanding of them.

opera: Italian, German, French, English and Russian. Opera, for those who lack the all-important context, can therefore become an endurance test on a grand scale, not too far removed from watching a cricket test match with no idea who is attempting to achieve what, let alone why. But even if we feel indifferent to the ambitious artistic vision an opera presents, or unmoved by the myths, legends and epic theatrical gestures that frequently underpin it, we can hardly fail to notice its potency.

Body Language

Body language, not unlike the language of music, clasps itself tightly to a unique cultural context and moment in time. There could be thousands of connotations to the simplest head nod, shake or bobble, for example. Though meaningful to some, our gestures inevitably appear inscrutable to others.

Visual signals between individuals play an indispensable role in so many walks of life, perhaps especially in sport. For example, in tennis doubles, players often appear to have evolved an elaborate system of communicating their intentions to each other based on body language and quick vocalizations. Musicians certainly need to interact in the

> 'Electric communication will never be a substitute
> for the face of someone who with their soul encourages
> another person to be brave and true.'
>
> Charles Dickens (1812–70)
> English writer and social critic

moment when playing as a group also, for there is a continual need to interpret each other's idiosyncratic gestures, body movements and facial expressions.

How do pop, folk, blues or jazz musicians customize the language of music to communicate meaning? My feeling is that in these forms the visual component becomes even more central and tangled up with the music itself – in other words, musical language and body language connect with any number of other significant cultural touchpoints. In many such examples, there may be lyrics with which to help convey a narrative less ambiguously, too. Frequently, the heartfelt message behind a love song seems reinforced by the singer's facial expression and physicality – even by the way they manipulate the microphone or make use of subdued lighting. The emotional-visual impact of, say, Al Jolson, Adele or Whitney Houston would seem to be an offshoot of their compelling stage presence – even with the volume turned down, we can hardly fail to appreciate what is being communicated. Perhaps the best example of all is gospel singing, where an unparalleled level of personal and collaborative conviction appears to transport the music onto another level of meaning altogether. Importantly, too, an audience's collective sense of engagement in the performance may well feed back directly in a rather powerful way. In this sense, the language of music perhaps inches a little closer to being a genuine exchange, at least in terms of the shared emotional message.

Actions Speak Louder Than Words

Examples of body language for performing musicians include nodding and head-tilting, a whole gamut of hand gesticulations and motions of the upper body, inward breathing to coincide with musical upbeats, and watching each other like hawks to ensure the precise placement of important rhythmic details. A good choir breathes as one, and a polished orchestra somehow manages to look and sound greater than the sum of its parts. Even a half-smile or arched eyebrow can have a variety of possible musical connotations, depending upon the context. Some of these cues are instrument-specific, such as the ways a violinist might lift or re-engage her bow, or how a pianist or percussionist might appear to 'conduct' himself by various refinements of wrist-lifting. Orchestral conductors need to be masters of non-verbal

Street-savvy Musicians

I have become increasingly impressed by the body language of street musicians, for whom an ability to coordinate what they are doing runs in parallel with their need to be projecting and engaging with an audience that is often indifferent and in transit. A vital component within the subtle chemistry and body language for performers of all types is an ability to listen intently – if there is an equivalent to 20:20 vision in sound, accomplished musicians have it.

communication – for their art may appear to take the form of a sophisticated, partly pre-choreographed dance; arguably though, a conductor's work is largely done beforehand during rehearsals, when the players are given ample opportunity to map each gesture onto a verbalized explanation.

Visual signals are invaluable for rock, folk and jazz groups too; playing in a tightly unified way is certainly not just a preoccupation for classical musicians. The lead guitarists in rock groups (David Lee Roth of the heavy rock group Van Halen and Pete Townsend of The Who spring to mind) signal important structural moments in their music by leaping gazelle-like into the air and pulling off an impressive 'back-scissors' kick. This places a sort of visual exclamation mark into the music, enabling it to fulfil something close to what classical performers do routinely when placing long, dramatic trills at perfect cadences. Interestingly, in a musical performance, visual exchanges between performers can also help an audience to pick up the connections between physical and musical gestures. But not all body language needs to be visible in order to have impact. Even from a recording, one can often detect the members of a string quartet breathing, or groaning, perhaps to heighten a particular kind of musical inflection or affectation. By such means we, the audience, are being communicated to directly; we do not feel incidental to the process, but woven into it importantly somehow, and hence come away sensing we have played an indispensable role in the music-making itself.

The Printed Page

Music manuscript resembles a treasure map, of sorts; indeed, its most potent clues often reward a little extra patience and insight. Each yellowing page from a rumbustious symphony remains strangely silent – until, finally, those intriguing dashes and squiggles leap majestically into musical life.

For those who read sheet music (widely known as 'modern staff notation'), the most compelling indicator that music can function as a language might appear to be its physical appearance in manuscript. For although conventions have changed dramatically since the very earliest symbol-based incarnations of music notation (things called 'neumes') many centuries ago, notation readers of any nationality will today usually be able to make sense of detailed markings when confronted with the same printed page of music. In modern notation, various forms happily coexist side by side, some geared optimally for jazz or classical music, others created more as a form of prompt/shorthand, or what is sometimes known as a 'lead sheet'. For example, the 'Nashville Number System' is a bespoke form of notation devised specifically with country music session players in mind, and many non-classical guitarists play from a system called 'tablature' (or 'tab'). Sometimes music is notated specifically to help performers fathom the idiosyncrasies of a particular composer's experimental music, for example the American avant-garde composer John Cage, who was among the first to modify the piano to create an array of strange buzzes, timbres and effects.

But the printed page is just one among many starting points from which meaningful music might emerge; African drummers, rock musicians and Chinese folk singers seem to do rather well without it. In some cases, it is the composer who appears to have thrown a spanner in the works, either by doing something different from what he had previously sanctioned in print, or by leaving open fundamental questions that may befuddle generations of editors and performers. What this all suggests is that even the score, which is at best a fixed though imperfect expression of the composer's intentions, is far from constituting a language. Though it is certainly possible to scribble music or words onto a page, in each case there will be the need to read between the lines and to search out something meaningful. This is where interpretation comes in.

Interpreting the Black Stuff

Composing is not just a matter of painting by numbers. And yet, were it not for a musician's practised skills of deciphering, music notation would remain just a jumble of self-important hieroglyphics. Regardless of how loosely or precisely music appears to have been notated, the task of turning all those impressive-looking dots and swirls into music comes down to the performer, who must weigh up his or her own interpretive options in light of what the composer appears to have been wanting. Hence, reading music from the page can never be merely a matter of faithful reproduction, just as writing it down will invariably require a significant amount of compromise on the composer's part. For these reasons, there will always be as many versions of a piece of music as there are interpreters. Incidentally, the same is true when we read words from a page: the voice sounding in your head will be different from mine; so will its pace, tone and characterization. The subtlest of pauses we might elect to place before a word serves to heighten its importance, for example, and the same is frequently true in music. Furthermore, since a composer communicates in ink and the player through sound, the terms of reference are straight away open to a good deal of slippage and inconsistency. Every accumulated hour a musician spends practising with a score in front of him is to some extent an attempt to objectify both it and the music it represents. The 'real' music lies concealed, waiting for the moment its various possible meanings can emerge. The listener, on the other hand, who has not been eavesdropping on the practising, hears the playing as a one-off experience; subjective, creative and temporarily definitive of the player's imagination.

Emotional Meaning

Music interpretation does not have to have anything to do with reading from manuscript – the ever-adaptable improviser Harry The Piano, for instance, would sooner learn a Mozart sonata by listening to recordings than from a score. However, interpretation will invariably have a great deal to do with individuality: 'When someone speaks, we hear the tone of voice rather than the words spoken'(from the CD sleeve *The Gestalt Approach*, recorded by pianist Emre Şen). Individuality, creativity and emotion may at times seem barely distinguishable from each other, but this is where a performer's personal involvement, or sense of 'ownership', really comes into play. Spontaneity must surely be allowed to function alongside what a performer may have previously learned about a particular piece. On the other hand, much conservatoire-level teaching (not just for classical musicians, incidentally, but also jazz and session players) starts from the assumption that the performer should be aiming to be more objective about what they are hoping to communicate. One may even be able to detect something faintly resembling method acting when looking at how some players go about honing their performing skills, whereby a kind of 'emotion memory' kicks in to substitute for genuine spontaneity.

It is certainly true that classical performers sometimes risk tipping into the realm of reinvention – bit by bit, the original work can become squeezed out by the sheer weight of on-the-spot decisions. When in 'performance mode', musicians often find that pace and poetry tug them in opposite directions. Hence a performer's ongoing artistic challenge is considerable: to keep a sense of balance and perspective; to play the music, not merely play *with* the music. Arguably, if a performer becomes overly wrapped up in what they are doing, the music will have a tendency to become self-indulgent and consequently less compelling to listen to. Similarly, when a performer becomes too free-spirited, the playing can sound breathless and unyielding, perhaps especially with classical and jazz music, but, it strikes me, also in heavy metal rock, as well as in some more florid forms of instrumental folk music.

Interpretation might also take the form of a cover version of a well-known pop, jazz or folk song. Here a rather different array of choices presents itself to a performer than when the starting point is the black-and-white appearance in some kind of score. One could be aiming to mimic the expressive inflections of the original singer, perhaps, or to be somewhat bolder and attempt a wholesale rethink of the song, for example from a slow ballad to a jaunty reggae version, or vice versa. Additionally, a singer might subsequently reinterpret their own song, perhaps by making it more impactful for a live setting – or by doing the opposite, as Eric Clapton did in his intimate acoustic live album of 1992, *Unplugged*.

Sensing & Expressing

I think it is important to distinguish between sensing an emotion and expressing something that has an emotional basis. Surely we can 'hear' the tears of expression in, for example, Elton John's 'Candle in the Wind', without him feeling any obligation to break down in the recording studio. The trouble with emotion is that it is not often a stable commodity. Hence, what a performer feeds back to him or herself in the moment will rarely be a reliable barometer of the emotional impact for an audience. Besides, surely the performer's task is to move other people, not to move himself.

The audience, on the other hand, can be permitted to be as emotional as it wishes – for listening is, of course, itself a form of interpretation. Importantly, each listener will arrive at their own nuanced meaning for every piece of music they encounter – there is no such thing as collective emotion (except possibly mass hysteria), however unanimous the response in a large auditorium may appear to be.

Performers and listeners often find themselves latching on to certain surface details in a song or piece of music, such as a saxophone solo or a particular line of words. However, it seems likely that the originator – who could equally well be Fats Waller, Wagner or Fatboy Slim – would have wanted us to scratch a little deeper and permit the music itself to ooze out. Our desire to pick away at those things we notice first, either from a score or a recording, can end up crushing the deeper emotional message into paste.

'Music is the shorthand of emotion.'

From *The Living Corpse*
Leo Tolstoy (1828–1910)
Russian writer

Silence Is Golden

Mindfulness practitioners know that mind-wandering is the polar opposite of what they are trying to achieve. By silencing the mind's continual impulse to wander and chatter away, we become calmer, and consequently better able to focus. So this is essentially about inner silence.

But there are different kinds of silence – Adam Ford in *The Art of Mindful Silence* explores several approaches – and my own experience as a pianist, performing on stages of different sizes, leaves me in no doubt regarding the existence of meaningful silence. There is the so-called 'pin drop' silence, a much-cherished commodity for any performer, especially when delivering music of extreme pathos. And then there is another – equally desirable – kind of silence that affects musicians of any discipline: I call it the 'silence of engagement'. Surely there are as many types of silence as there are occasions we experience it, for example when a cathedral choir has just finished evensong, or as a trumpeter prepares to play the 'Last Post' at a Remembrance Day service; and how about those magical few seconds of silence that can occur before the applause starts at a pop concert, directly after a particularly soulful ballad has ended? Perhaps in such circumstances we learn more about our individual response to silence than silence itself.

Silence Is Music

John Cage's *4'33"* is a piece of conceptual music composed in 1952, which, while not celebrating silence as such, goes some way to upholding the value of noises off. No notes are required to be played throughout, and any line-up of instruments can be employed (since the 'musical' outcome will of course be the same, regardless). Just as is the case with any conventional musical performance, each one is still destined to be different; it is our awareness of how the time passes that partly defines each occasion – and, of course, the ever-changing environmental effect. Cage's point was that the only thing common to both sound and silence is the time each soaks up. *4'33"* does not really constitute a lesson in how to listen *per se*, and yet it is remarkably revealing of the role audiences play within the grander musical experience.

Some think that death is what gives meaning to life. By the same token, silence may be the only thing that gives meaning to sound, hence music. It seems paradoxical that outer space is inconceivably large, and yet at the same time as silent as a single atom in our fingernail. We are enchanted by the very notion of silence, and yet no living human being has ever truly experienced it.

'Music expresses that which cannot be put into words
and that which cannot remain silent.'

FROM *WILLIAM SHAKESPEARE*
VICTOR HUGO (1802–85), FRENCH WRITER

A CONSPIRACY OF SILENCE

Why not give your own performance of Cage's *4'33"* – while sitting under your beloved cherry tree, or on a family outing in the car? Explain in a few words what will happen, perform the piece, and then take a moment to talk about what each of you experienced.

The Language of Emotion

On balance, there is perhaps as much music in language as there is language in music; for both music and language tend to evolve slowly out of complex overlapping conventions. My overarching point in this chapter is that these two modes of communication – music and language – hardly ever meet in the middle, however convenient some of us think it would be if they did. Aside from Morse Code, we have few direct means of communicating via sound available to us. One problem with thinking of music as a language is that, by implication, many people will feel they are not fluent in that language – that there's a party going on to which they have not been invited. Instead of searching for some improbable 'literal' meaning in music, surely we would be better off simply enjoying it for what it is: a boundless creative repository of human emotion. However well music is able to communicate a particular emotion, it makes little sense to imagine it functions anything like a language. Babies move easily to music (even 'complex' classical music) and YouTube is groaning under the strain of videos featuring animals responding to music, or even playing it. No amount of evolution will ever turn music into a kind of universally comprehensible Esperanto.

There is perhaps as much music in language as language in music

But enough of what music is not. For what we are left with is of course infinitely more gainful – music is the language of engagement *par excellence*, a pinpoint on the map of humanity where the lines of expression and emotion finally converge, and where imagination counts for at least as much as knowledge. Music, when all's said and done, is there to heighten the senses – to be 'felt' – not to be forensically prised open and gawped at. Music should not be considered a frivolity or a utility. Nor is its contract with humanity fulfilled the moment a composer finally rests his pen, or a singer inches away from her microphone. Any communicating that is done presupposes some level of engagement by us: in short, a willingness to be communicated to.

'Music is the soul of language.'

MAX HEINDEL (1865–1919)
DANISH-AMERICAN ASTROLOGER AND MYSTIC

CHAPTER FIVE

PARALLEL UNIVERSES

Could there be more to music than meets the ear? From embracing music as a motivational aid to craving it as a tranquillizer, many of us feel we need music in order to help us function. But what is happening to us, physically and emotionally, when we experience music? It is as if our imagination has been consigned to inhabit a parallel universe, certainly one that has little to do with what we can see, touch, smell, taste – or indeed hear.

Music's Otherworldliness

To be moved and mesmerized by beautiful sounds is to be human. In music we can find solace and inspiration aplenty; though born into the material world, we look to music for inspiration to help us reach beyond its more obvious dimensions.

OUR MODERN WORLD teems with sound. Some of it is music; the rest, as the American music critic Alex Ross enlightened us in 2007, is noise. The fact that we all seem hardwired to perceive the same piece of music in wholly different ways surely contributes to its magical ambiguity – and therefore, its otherworldliness. One need only listen to Vaughan Williams's *Five Mystical Songs*, or indeed any of the 'mystical' piano sonatas composed by his contemporary, Alexander Scriabin, to gain a sense of how music has the power to transport us to somewhere random and fantastical. The only limiting factor, it would seem, is us. And yet, if we listen to the Czech composer Janáček's *On an Overgrown Path* – an exquisite collection of piano pieces composed to evoke a personal spiritual journey – the music could hardly contrast more with, say, the Hindustani music of the Sufi teacher Hazrat Inayat Khan. Khan's creative energy emanates from mystical vibrations and a concept of teaching defined as 'wazifa'.

Some might argue that all music is otherworldly if it comes from the hand of a human being, though by that token, Mozart could conceivably count as an early existentialist. And then there

> 'The power of the word which works upon each atom of the body, making it sonorous, making it a medium of communication between the external life and the inner life.'
>
> From *The Mysticism of Sound and Music*
> Hazrat Inayat Khan (1882–1927)

are those who appear equally confident that all enduring music descends directly from God. But once we've started down this path, perhaps we are in danger of attempting to define spirituality, not music. A more mindful view might be that 'earth music' counts as the purest form of music of all – a fox scurrying from a hedge-row, perhaps, or the rhythmic rat-a-tat of a distant woodpecker.

From out of the earliest civilizations, and throughout more recent centuries also, composers and musicians from all walks of life have clung tightly to otherworldliness. This is probably because it opens up a panoply of possibilities, ranging from the creational to the supernatural. Ironically, in musical terms, death (or more usually the faint prospect of afterlife, transfiguration or reincarnation) has tended to feature more prominently than life, almost irrespective of genre: Queen's 'Bohemian Rhapsody' and Purcell's 'Dido's Lament' immediately spring to mind. The metaphysics of music lies at its very heart – indeed, one could even say that music is all about the connection it makes with our heart. From the earliest times, mystics from the Far East sensed that sound was at the root of all physical creation – in other words, certain sounds were responsible for bringing shape, order and proportion to the objects we see all around us. Moreover, in Christian, Jewish and Hindu texts we often find allusions to divine speech, not just in its meaning but in the utterance of the words itself.

Sixth Sense

Have you ever wondered whether you have a sixth sense? Many people feel they are at times able to detect something oddly intangible, invisible and inaudible, and yet the experience of which seems palpably 'real'. Music, one could argue, affects us this way all the time – which is precisely why we welcome it into our lives. And yet, while sometimes we feel we possess the panoramic vision of a bird in low flight, at other times the world we inhabit seems strangely aloof.

We cannot rely on our five senses alone to make sense of what we are experiencing

We all know that music can help us to feel certain emotions – we might, for example, put on a loud, up-tempo piece of music as we are getting dressed up to attend a party, or seek out a tranquil track by the Irish singer-songwriter Enya when we have kicked off our work shoes. We are just getting 'in the mood'. But is it possible there is some reason, also associated with sound, why we sometimes feel unaccountably troubled, down or in conflict with ourselves? According to the British philosopher

Barry Smith, who I heard speaking on the BBC Radio 4 series *Uncommon Senses*, it is possible that our assumption that the brain is always the driver of what we feel or sense is not necessarily true. He poses the question of whether the body might to a degree know what it feels even before the brain does. This is not so much about dabbling in reverse logic as daring to think about the 'sense' behind sensation, or perhaps to reconsider how the body itself reacts, whether positively or negatively, especially to certain sound stimuli.

Clearly, we cannot rely on our five senses alone to make sense of what we are experiencing. For example, a 'sixth sense' could explain the feeling that someone is standing close behind us, so-called phantom limbs, sense of direction, ball sense and sense of balance, the experience of localized pain, or what time of the day it is. Then of course there is a sense of perspective, a sense of impending doom – or even a sense of humour. What on earth (or beyond it) is common sense, or a sense of occasion? In more specifically musical terms, there is the sense of pitch, the all-important sense of rhythm and time; in mindfulness, we treasure the sense of self, of now, of inner peace.

Infrasonic Sound

There is reason to believe that infrasonic sounds – those emitted below about 20 Hz, the lowest a healthy young person is able to detect – might cause us to feel uneasy, or even downright scared. Something sensed, or in a way 'understood' by our body in this way may not ever get an opportunity to become computed or reconciled by our conscious brain. Hence, though we may feel weirdly out of sorts, we are unable to put our finger on the issue. I recall feeling something faintly disturbing when travelling on the Paris Metro, and wondering whether the deep rumbling sensation coming at me from all around, pulsating in and out in waves, was responsible for the progressively disquieting, numbing sensations I was experiencing. Though for me these strange feelings never amounted to paranoia, I can conceive of how some people might be affected in such a way.

There can be an upside to infrasonic sounds, though – organ builders have long had a penchant for incorporating massive piping for the deepest notes, and one can really sense something majestic and awe-inspiring when a 64-foot pipe is being used in a cathedral or auditorium, such as the largest pipe organ ever built, the Boardwalk Hall Auditorium Organ in Atlantic City, New Jersey. We don't just hear its lower resonances, we feel them physically come to life through the floor. If the physical manifestations of the simplest sound can affect how our body is feeling even before it has had a chance to alter our state of mind, one wonders what might this tell us about the possibilities bound up in complex music?

MUSIC: A JOURNEY THROUGH TIME

It is often said that truth is stranger than fiction. And yet, curiously, the untold mysteries of the real world – and real time – generally appear less alluring to musicians and storytellers. If speculation is the engine of creativity, mystery is the stuff of legend-makers.

THE IDEA of time travel, and journeying through space, is of undying fascination for us. Perhaps we all have a little of George Orwell's intrepid spirit living in us, urging us to contemplate the world a century on. It occurs to me that we might find it even harder to make sense of the real world if we did not have the possibility, however abstract, of some means of escaping from it. This might take the form of a time machine in the H. G. Wells mould, *Star Trek, Doctor Who*, or else some musical evocation, such as Rick Wakeman's 'Journey to the Centre of the Earth', an epic progressive rock piece from 1974 that I recall frightened the living daylights out of me when I first heard it as a teenager.

A musician's take on interplanetary or time travel is potentially every bit as illuminating and thought-provoking as the apocryphal words of a literary master, such as Douglas Adams's eternally humorous *A Hitchhiker's Guide to the Galaxy*, of 1978. Take, for example, Gustav Holst's *The Planets*, composed between 1914 and 1916, a work that may appear to be as much about the interrelationships between the planets – spatially, spiritually and even astrologically – as the essential physical attributes of any one of them. We are right to be intrigued by parallel universes, the fantastical possibilities of quantum physics and the mystical properties of the unproven, for without them our journey to work and our endless circumnavigations of the supermarket would seem all the more humdrum. It is not just children who crave the possibility of impossibility in books like Lewis Carroll's *Alice's Adventures in Wonderland* or the 'Harry Potter' series – adults too need to slip off into space now and again, be it with the help of David Bowie's 'Life on Mars' or 'Echo Beach' by Martha and the Muffins. Music does not just validate our musings about time travel or journeying somewhere mystical, it can itself provoke such ideas. In the nineteenth century, the concept of the wanderer, earnestly searching for his or her inner self, preoccupied the German poet Johann Wolfgang von Goethe and the Hungarian composer Franz Liszt, who became progressively fascinated by pilgrimages. Music's ability to

'Man … can go up against gravitation in a balloon, and why should he not hope that ultimately he may be able to stop or accelerate his drift along the Time-Dimension, or even turn about and travel the other way.'

FROM *THE TIME MACHINE*
H. G. WELLS (1866–1946), ENGLISH WRITER

transport us to somewhere more interesting and enlightening than we are right now, or else to ease the journey itself, is for many people justification alone for its existence.

Out of This World

Were it not for the existence of the creative-inquisitive mind, there might be little point in giving the notion of time travel, Tardises or time capsules more than a second's serious consideration. In *A Christmas Carol,* for example, Charles Dickens dares to contemplate time travel both backwards and forwards, while a cleverly confusing repositioning of 'now' is just as meaningfully captured in the films *Sliding Doors* and *Pulp Fiction*. Operas and musicals frequently make play of shifting time zones, too – for example, the use of Shakespeare's *Taming of the Shrew*, which functions as a play within a play in Cole Porter's *Kiss Me, Kate*. It would seem music can place us in a different time in just a few notes, without any need for pyrotechnics, strobe lighting or theatrical mist.

For me, the haunting sound of Gregorian chant carries with it a musty antiquity. And, for many listeners, Richard Strauss's Nietzsche-inspired tone poem *Also sprach Zarathustra*, composed in 1896, immediately conjures up Stanley Kubrick's epic science-fiction film *2001: A Space Odyssey* (1968), in which daring juxtapositions of time and space rise up through the music every bit as powerfully as the intriguing black structure that pops up oddly throughout the film.

Admittedly, such fantastical notions are not infrequently connotations we ourselves impose, and which do not necessarily function within the music itself. And yet the soundtrack to the film *Back to the Future* by American composer Alan Sylvestri is surely a masterful evocation of time travel by anyone's measure. Music can help us to slide daringly from one world to another, not unlike Lucy's wardrobe transition into Narnia in C. S. Lewis's 'Chronicles'. An incongruous baroque flavour injected into a pop song can achieve something faintly similar. Examples would be 'Golden Brown' by the Stranglers, which works simply by adding a harpsichord into an otherwise conventional rock band line-up, or The Beatles' 'Penny Lane', featuring a piccolo trumpet, or ELO's 'Mr Blue Sky', which combines a vocoded (synthetic) voice with eighteenth-century strings to magnificent effect.

NEPTUNE: THE FURTHEST PLANET

Listen to Holst's 'Neptune' from *The Planets*. 'Neptune, the Mystic' is the result of the English composer's lifelong fascination with astrology and theosophy. One cannot help but connect the ethereal sound of female off-stage voices with the theme music to the TV series *Star Trek*, though in most other respects these two musical evocations could hardly contrast more.

How High the Moon?

It is not just philosophers, astrologers and astronomers who continue to be fascinated by the moon. For beyond its unmistakable effect on tides, the moon's magnetic allure also lies in its seductive power over artists, poets and musicians of all descriptions.

In music, cows can jump over the moon, vampires are summoned and werewolves become instantly empowered – rumour even has it that there is a man living up there. Pink Floyd's album of 1973, *The Dark Side of the Moon*, remains delightfully enigmatic, full of oblique references and darker moments. Some believe that on the day of the new moon we experience a heightened level of mental activity that is 'darker' or in some way sinister. We also have half-moons, waxing moons, blue moons and even moon rivers – all of these have at various times provided fodder for writers, thinkers and perhaps especially musicians. The moon appears to have influenced many composers, albeit more obliquely at times – Dvořák's *Song to the Moon* and Stanford Robinson's *Moonmaiden's Dance* immediately come to mind. The Italian baroque composer Antonio Vivaldi wrote a concerto for flute entitled *La Notte*, the individual movements of which seem to be alluding to the various phases of the moon. 'Moonshadow' by Cat Stevens has a more consistently jaunty feel to it. While 'Fly Me to the Moon' is quite possibly the most popular song involving the

'Music is the moonlight in the gloomy night of life.'

From *Titan*
Jean Paul (1763–1825)
GERMAN WRITER

moon, Beethoven's *Moonlight* Sonata of 1801 is almost certainly the most famous musical example of all. Disappointingly, perhaps, the composer did not give the music any such title, though he did give it quite a provocative subtitle: 'Quasi una fantasia' ('In the manner of a fantasy'). As was common in music throughout the nineteenth century, it was a German music critic (in this case, Ludwig Rellstab) who suggested the nickname 'Moonlight', but only some thirty years after the music was composed. I think we can all agree that the title 'Op. 27 No. 2 in C sharp minor' is alarmingly hygienic compared with Rellstab's poetic suggestion.

Upon First Hearing the 'Moonlight' Sonata

I do not fully recall what it was that first drew me towards Beethoven's *Moonlight* Sonata. I suppose it may have been a desire to lock horns with its odd 'triplety' appearance on the page. But in all probability it was the music's intoxicating power to communicate something neither Beethoven nor I could ever hope to express in any number of words. As a small boy, I spent many hours doodling at the piano, guided only by the faint slivers of moonlight between the curtains. I quickly developed a knack for switching from improvising back to practising the instant I heard my parents coming upstairs. To this day, I regularly enjoy passing on the skill of improvisation to music teachers.

I have no doubt that my doodling revealed more to me about the *Moonlight* Sonata's mystical qualities than any amount of navel-gazing about its clever semiotics, or sifting through the black stuff dotted about its pages. Such earth-bound attributes ultimately just get in the way of the music's transcendental powers, even for pianists who make a point of regularly revisiting the piece. If it suits you to picture moonlight shimmering over Lake Lucerne, I can't imagine Beethoven would have objected, regardless of whether the thought ever actually occurred to him, as Rellstab fancifully suggested. After all, the natural world was almost certainly something Beethoven prized as highly as humanity – he once reflected that he generally preferred the company of a tree to that of a man. Listening or playing through the *Moonlight* now, for perhaps the thousandth time, I feel entirely free from any impulse to overthink it or pick at it with a sharpened pencil. Though I could analyse the living daylights out of its 69 bars, I choose instead to let its inner secrets live on without further judgement. It's a bit like finally trusting myself to swim without armbands; something fresh and new is born out of its familiar tumbling tune every time I return to it. I am completely persuaded by its meditative power.

CHAPTER SIX

THE ART OF POSSIBILITY

Mindfulness and music hold a mirror to the life we have so far led. At the same time, they propel us forwards into the future. Keeping excited about what we are doing in our daily lives takes a certain amount of investment and self-investigation. Ironically, too much soul-searching just leaves us wounded and worn out. Our commitment to feeling satisfied and engaged needs to be ongoing and adaptable; how willing we are to explore the art of possibility says a lot about who we are right now.

Another String to Your Bow

There is immeasurable pleasure to be gained from being an astute, attentive listener; yet when a person takes up a musical instrument, the bond between them quickly becomes like no other. I sometimes feel I'm able to detect bits of my personality tangled up in the strings of my piano.

In my early years as Assistant Director of Music at a school in Somerset, England, I would engage from time to time with my fellow teachers in a faintly dubious musical challenge: we would set about learning (I feel a cringe coming on as I recall this) a new musical instrument in the shortest time imaginable. An incentive would take the form of seeing our names entered for a music exam – say, Grade 3 on the clarinet or French horn – with perhaps a week or less in which to prepare. What started as the crazy buffoonery of impetuous young staff, already jaded by the imminent prospect of yet another season of wall-to-wall carol services, would turn out to be a strangely exhilarating annual experience. Though I am reluctant to recommend such an absurdly immersive method of learning a musical instrument – not least because of the somewhat shallow level of accomplishment it inevitably resulted in – I would nevertheless reflect that it was well worth the effort. If for no other reason, these experiences always brought home to me the anguish felt by the pupils as they were being put through their paces.

> 'It's easy to play any instrument:
> all you have to do is touch the right key at the right
> time and the instrument will play itself.'
>
> J. S. Bach (1685–1750)
> GERMAN COMPOSER

I am sometimes asked how far a keen adult beginner might conceivably be able to advance with a musical instrument. It might sound as though I'm dodging the question, but my best response is that it really doesn't matter. It's all about the satisfaction, friendships and unanticipated benefits we gain while trying. It's also about the improved mindfulness we can acquire simply by embarking on our own voyage of discovery, moving steadily forwards and building in confidence with every step. More realistic questions a prospective musician might ask herself are these: how much pleasure can I hope to gain from hearing myself make a wonderful sound on a euphonium, and what might I be able to learn about myself in the process?

Motivation & Obsession

What motivates you in your musical life? Is it the feeling of camaraderie you gain from playing trombone in a ska band, or do you consider yourself more of a discerning listener? Perhaps it is the collective success you enjoy as you stand shoulder to shoulder with fellow singers, or the joy you get from attending concerts with

TAKE UP A MUSICAL INSTRUMENT

Why not have a go at learning to play the saxophone, or pick up where you left off with that long-discarded double bass languishing in the loft? Will anyone judge you if you make a sound like a wardrobe being dragged across the kitchen floor? We listen to professional musicians for the pleasure of something enticingly beautiful, but we do not necessarily need to have such lofty ambitions when we take up an instrument (or perhaps return to it) later in life. Music does not always need to be a spectator sport. Just think of the advantage you may gain from preserving your hand-eye coordination, mobility and vital motor skills, the sense of achievement that can come from playing a melody you have always longed to hear yourself play, or the incontestable satisfaction of gaining a thumbs-up from the teenager next door. You may even feel inclined to do things properly and find yourself a teacher to help chart your progress. There is mounting evidence to suggest that learning an instrument can stave off dementia – or perhaps postpone it for a while – and once you can play a little more reliably, a whole panorama of possibilities will open up for you: playing duets with friends, or accompanying an occasional hymn in church.

friends who love the same kinds of music. The key to reaching the 'pleasure point' for the practising musician is to keep motivated; for the listener also, there is the need to feel optimistic and engaged with the music others are making. The relationship between fun and function in music can be an uneasy one: music always deserves our energy, either in order to play it or to listen to it. It is important to be enjoying the process of whatever it is we are doing, not forever speculating, churning over or 'end-gaming', as Frederick Alexander so aptly termed it. Enjoyment and fulfilment come in the moment, and that moment all too quickly melts into the past.

The pursuit of success, however we may choose to measure it, certainly carries with it an inclination to act with purpose and determination. It takes real commitment, energy and stoicism to rise above the obstacles life can place in our path. The irony is that those who love music can easily end up being hurt by it. For the practising musician, this presents something of a conundrum: the objectives of mindfulness – to be calm, not preoccupied by what is around the corner or condemning of our perceived shortcomings – and the driving force of our inner motivation to accomplish certain things. When I was at music college, the practising habits of some of my cohort seemed perilously close to obsessive – one friend clocked up over eight hours per day on a regular basis, yet achieved negligibly more than the rest of us, who spent more time nursing a pint than memorizing Mozart. The point at which one's drive to progress drifts into obsessive micromanagement is perhaps different for each of us; hence, the solution to it will be different, too. According to Malcolm Gladwell in his book *Outliers: The Story of Success*, most people who achieve mastery in something, whether it be golf or music, will need to put in around 10,000 hours. If you are the kind of person who feels the need to toil away at the nitty-gritty on a musical instrument, motivated solely by a desire to reach the next level, you will perhaps not flinch at this statistic. Others might regard this degree of focus unhealthy or unbalanced. After all, a mere 9,000 hours might be more than enough for your needs, particularly if it frees up 1,000 hours for brushing up on your Spanish, learning to swim or helping out in your local community.

THE TIPPING POINT

When it comes to the question of motivation versus obsession, some of us eventually arrive at a tipping point. We need to keep our longer-term ambitions in check if we are learning an instrument, and amateur learners seem equally at risk of losing a sense of proportion. This is not because many will have eight hours a day to devote to playing or singing, but because learning a particular piece, or targeting an event such as an exam, can take over a musician's life and squeeze out the sense of enjoyment or fulfilment. As a teacher, I have seen this kind of overly zestful determination many times among highly motivated adult players. The end result can range from a temporary sense of underachievement to a longer term feeling of inadequacy, the latter leading some to give up learning altogether – even those who exhibit terrific potential. If a

> 'Endeavour to play easy pieces well and with elegance; that is better than to play difficult pieces badly.'
>
> Robert Schumann (1810–56)
> German Composer

Keeping in the Loop

Rarely will the advice we give ourselves equal the quality of insight others around us can offer. Once lost, a sense of perspective can be hard to re-establish. It is a good idea to make regular connections with fellow musicians, or, if appropriate, to invest in an occasional consultation lesson with someone you trust. This can help to keep you moving forwards at a rate you are able to sustain.

musician is self-taught, the situation can slip out of control even more quickly, since there is no voice of reason to help steer the person back into a healthier state of mind.

Make a Mindful Difference

If you do not play an instrument, or sing, the motivation needed to keep your love of music buoyant can still be something that needs bolstering from time to time. After all, mindfulness in music is as much about keeping you connected with yourself as keeping you connected to an instrument. It is important to value the contribution you can make to keeping music a vibrant component in your life; life without music might not be unimaginable, but it is certainly likely to be less colourful. Almost irrespective of where you live, there will be opportunities for you to integrate valuably with the music scene – or indeed, to get one going. The fact that you are reading this book indicates you almost certainly have something robust to bring to your musical community, whether it be volunteering your services as a steward at a concert hall, helping to organize or raise funds for local shows, musicals or pantomimes, leading musical walks for the University of the Third Age, or popping into your nearby school to demonstrate what a theremin sounds like. You may also have thought of ways you can thread mindfulness valuably into the lives of friends and loved ones by connecting its broader messages with your passion for music. Reinvention is how we value what we already have. It is also the engine of our onward journey. This can be especially the case if we find we suddenly have a gap to fill in our lives and a little energy going spare. The commitment to music you have is infectious – spread it freely. Whatever it may have been that first awoke in you a passion for music is perhaps a good way for you to feed something back in, for it clearly touched you in an enduring and meaningful way.

The Gift of Music

It sometimes occurs to us to buy driving or flying lessons as presents, and at one point the gift of a hot-air balloon ride for couples celebrating wedding anniversaries became almost a cliché. Why not ring the changes by purchasing your loved one a few guitar lessons, or send them on a musical retreat? You never know, it might turn out to be the gift of a lifetime.

Make Stuff Up

Improvising on a musical instrument is perhaps less of a skill, more of an impulse. Improvising is not unlike the approach an impressionist artist takes when charcoaling a landscape; in each case we end up with something intentionally sketchy, yet 'complete'.

Improvisation works equally well as a collaborative or solo experience; it presents a welcome opportunity to declutter the mind. Improvising also stymies our impulse to correct, backtrack or evaluate; we learn to reward ourselves in the moment and then simply move on. It is true that when we shoot from the hip, we can generally expect to be a little less accurate – but we'll undoubtedly be a whole lot quicker on the draw. Improvising gives the non-reading musician licence to make spontaneous, attractive music on the fly. For the score buff, it stimulates creative areas of the 'right' brain that Beethoven can never reach. A musician's mind is an emporium of sound – a place where colour and nuance, fact and fantasy, past and present blur majestically into one another. Venturing off-piste now and again, with whatever instrument is to hand – even a couple of spoons – feels like going into musical free fall. Improvising does not have to have anything to do with jazz, nor does it need to turn into a memorable event for other people (though it may well become one for you, once you've got the hang of combining your improvising with mindful breathing).

For those who insist that music must always aspire to be a Fabergé egg in its immaculate form and symmetry, improvising presents the ultimate reality check. If composing music can be considered a high-end sophisticated activity, improvising is a reassuringly low-tech, hands-on craft. Actually, improvising is among the most illuminating things anyone can do with a musical instrument. It's essentially the difference between studiously following a recipe or going for the stir-fry option. Improvising is most definitely not 'kids' stuff', nor need it be something best left to 'other people'. It's simply a wonderful way of unleashing the creative you, no holds barred. If you can pull one note out of your imagination, you can surely add a second – and if you can string five together, you're well on the way to creating your first miniature improvisation piece. Look out through your window, breathe long and full, and let your music gush out.

Today, improvising at the piano seems as natural to me as breathing. Were I to find myself stuck on a desert island with just a piano and a volume of Clementi sonatas for company, I would lose no time in shredding most of it for kindling and lavatory paper, save a page or two for scribbling messages to stuff into bottles, and then spend my time surveying the horizon while improvising. I have no doubt that the skill of playing 'on the hoof' led naturally from my earliest experiences building up an aural map of whatever music I happened to be learning. In some form or another, improvisation has gone on to underpin much of my musical life ever since.

Improve Your Improv.

I have always greatly valued the virtual piano in my head; accessing it is a little like being able to hear conversations spoken in the voices of people I know well, engaging confidently, interrupting each other, and leaving a satisfying glow lingering in the memory. A firm trace of these musical conversations is left behind, ready to be resumed at any point. When one has access to imagined sound, it quickly becomes one's starting point for other mindful, musical activities. Creativity in music often seems to happen once we have been able to overturn previously held assumptions – for example, that music must always be in a particular key, or have a discernible pulse that people can tap their feet to. Improvising on a musical instrument does two things for us simultaneously: it encourages us to experiment in the here and now – itself a very mindful activity – and it helps us to savour the occasional spark of wisdom when we feel we've just had one. Improvising is akin to wandering down a long, narrow, dimly lit corridor of creativity; destination unknown, yet tentatively optimistic and impatient for connections. When things finally begin to click, we find ourselves glued to the instrument. It can also help us to be just a little more open to risk-taking when playing music written by other people. Actually, cultivating the skill of improvisation starts simply – with a single, rather beautiful note; it's like beginning a story with *Once upon a time...*

THE TALENT MYTH

Are you a late bloomer? Perhaps you have avoided taking up singing or playing an instrument simply because you were once told you lack the necessary talent? I'd like to unpack the word 'talent' a little further, to see if it's worth the paper it's written on.

When we have a hard time explaining some human phenomenon in terms of logic, or common sense, it seems we sometimes resort to shrugging it off as 'talent'. We don't think of a tall person as being talented for being tall, or a beautiful person for being beautiful; these are attributes, or good fortune perhaps, but not skills, talents or badges of honour. I've long had a bee in my bonnet when it comes to praising or acknowledging musical talent. Perhaps this is because I hear the term bandied about so glibly, occasionally from misguided parents, keen to kick-start their ten-year-old's CV on the basis of being able to struggle through a couple of tunes on the cello. If the cap appears to fit, rather like Cinderella's glass slipper, the talent mill just carries on turning unchallenged. On the one hand there is the irrefutable evidence of child prodigies, those whose early onset of remarkable skill testifies to genius status – Mozart, or in the modern age, the British musician Thomas Adès; there are many more examples. On the other hand, one detects the distant rumble of an assumption that secondary status should be conferred upon those who had to graft away in their musical endeavours in order to eventually achieve a comparable level of excellence. This could even include those who were themselves once credited with an appreciable amount of talent.

Musically Gifted – Fact or Fantasy?

I have yet to be persuaded that any plausible yardstick exists for assessing the musically gifted – we can certainly spot youngsters who already exhibit extraordinary ability, but not before they've had a chance to demonstrate it; we can also place an arbitrary age limit by which prodigal status needs to have been reached. But both criteria fail to detect similar abilities lying dormant in older people, or those of any age who, for whatever reason, were never able to come within reaching distance of a musical instrument. Music exams, competitions and festivals are there primarily to acknowledge and celebrate achievement – not to predict the future. There are of course those who display a physical aptitude for playing an instrument or singing, and some whose ease of coordination or mental agility would appear to give them a head start, but these are flimsy indicators of the potential to be more successful in the long run. Added to this is that although some of us may be fortunate enough to receive music lessons early, they may turn out to have been on the wrong instrument. On balance, surely there are other things that will impact greatly on how we turn out, such as our application, dedication or learning environment – not to mention the support we may be lucky enough to receive from those around us?

Talent Is Just a Word

The word 'talent' freezes out most of us in an instant – if not by intention, by default. Besides, faced with the existence of geniuses, it seems mere talent is not enough. There is no musical talent equivalent to IQ, though there have been tests that crudely attempted to pick out youngsters considered especially worthy of attention – for example, the Arnold Bentley 'Measures of Musical Abilities' (1966), widely regarded the benchmark in the UK and elsewhere for several decades. That musical geniuses have always existed is not in question, but the sheer speed by which they pick up their skills, and the comparatively slow pace others around them eventually acquire their own, is where any obvious advantage usually comes to a conspicuous halt. Prodigal status is perhaps not all it's cracked up to be – and I'm not just saying that because I was not one myself.

Crystal-ball gazing is undoubtedly made easier when a young child can already rattle off a fiendishly difficult riff on an electric guitar, or whizz through a Chopin étude on the piano, but an unintended consequence of placing them on a pedestal may be the underestimation of other potentially 'talented' class members at school. The well-documented halo effect has a great deal to answer for. For all you know, your hairdresser is the most musically talented person you have ever met; they almost certainly won't know it either. The word 'talent', therefore, is just that – a word, which holds back many and galvanizes only a handful. Since the absence of proof is not the proof of absence, I think it would be safer to assume we all have talent – or better still, stop using the term.

Failing the Litmus Test

A couple of areas that seem especially prone to being used as a litmus test of a person's musical talent (or lack thereof) are perfect pitch and its polar opposite, tone-deafness. The first is most certainly not a myth, although often misunderstood; the other is so rare, in my opinion, that it may as well be. Of one thing we can be sure: the vast majority of human beings do not have either.

PERFECT PITCH

Perfect pitch (or 'absolute' pitch, as it's sometimes referred to) is often mistaken to mean a variety of things, but usually being able to sing or play immaculately in tune. Among seasoned musicians, however, it is generally considered to be an aural phenomenon, not a practical skill. Perfect pitch is where a person (not necessarily a musician) is able automatically to detect the pitch of any particular note, or notes in a chord, thrown at them at random. They may well be able to replicate pitch precisely too, though in my experience this is not necessarily the case (I have known violinists with perfect pitch who seem to be playing out of tune for much of the time). The fact that most accomplished musicians sing or play in tune, and yet only .01 per cent of people are born with perfect pitch, should be evidence enough that perfect pitch has little to do with practical ability. (In fact, even those possessing perfect pitch would probably remain unaware they have it unless they take up singing or playing an instrument.) Many trained musicians find they have days when they possess something close to perfect pitch; alas, it is just a mirage, for the next day it has unaccountably disappeared again.

Actually, perfect pitch is often thought of (by those who have it) as a double-edged sword. On the positive side, it can greatly aid the precision of what a musician is routinely required to do, such as pluck notes reliably out of the air. On the other hand, it can be a poisoned chalice, because one's fellow musicians may not be similarly endowed, which means having to transpose the 'known' pitch to the one that prevails, adding another layer of complexity to what is being done. This can be particularly disconcerting when the unanimous shortcoming in pitch is less than a semitone, or when musicians play together at what is known as baroque tuning (i.e. 'flatter' than A=440 Hz). Conductors sometimes have perfect pitch, and there is fragile evidence to suggest that others of us can acquire it if we work progressively to build upon what is commonly called 'relative pitch'. Perfect pitch is something of a quirk, not a prerequisite to success in any field of music. Like synesthesia, it's either there or it's not, but either way, it's certainly not a deal-breaker. The next time someone informs you their daughter has perfect pitch, you might want to take it with a pinch of salt.

TONE-DEAFNESS

Definitions of tone-deafness vary from the uncharitable to the downright preposterous. Perhaps we would be less inclined to use the term so frivolously were it not for the known existence of its celebrated cousin, perfect pitch. My personal view is that tone-deafness exists about as rarely as perfect pitch; in human hearing terms, therefore, both phenomena should be considered outliers. No apparatus yet exists by which we can detect what is going on inside a person's head regarding their sense of pitch. Instead, we tend to assume that a person's apparent inability to reproduce a note on an instrument (or else to sing it back faithfully) constitutes proof they were unable to hear it accurately in the first place. This is almost certainly bogus, for singing and listening have, in my experience, relatively little to do with each other. Tone-deafness is not the aural equivalent to colour-blindness, which is a human condition one must learn to live with.

Most amateur choirs have what are ungenerously known as 'groaners' among their ranks who, on the face of it, fall into the category of tone-deaf. Their presence can indeed counter what is being achieved elsewhere in the group. But such a person is very likely still able to differentiate between good and bad singing. They will in many cases be capable of detecting mispitching in themselves and others, and hence gain satisfaction from listening to music that is well made. The shortcoming therefore almost certainly lies in the singing, not the hearing. As a music examiner, I have enjoyed listening to some 25,000 candidates worldwide, ranging from tiny tots who almost disappear behind their music stands to confident young adults on the cusp of a professional career. I can assure you that I have heard execrable singing emerge from the mouths of oboists and trumpeters who, two minutes earlier, played their pieces exquisitely.

SING FROM THE HILLTOPS

Has your singing voice been kept in a box all these years? Were you reprimanded as a child for being a groaner? If so, I warmly encourage you to reconsider your possibilities. It may be the case that singing – an avenue of music-making that places especially high demands on an ability to replicate pitch accurately – is not the optimum outlet for your musicianship. That said, even this might turn out to be a false assumption, for your voice may have been breaking or settling at the time you suffered the ignominy of being written off as a hopeless case, aged 13. Either way, this does not obviate you considering learning a whole raft of other instruments, such as percussion, harp, guitar, organ or piano, all of which call chiefly upon other musical skills and where a good sense of rhythm and coordination rise very much to the fore.

The Road Ahead

I hope you will arrive at these final pages with renewed vigour and optimism about the road that stretches ahead of you. We all own the music that underscores our existence. This confers upon us the right to consider how best to embrace music and the sounds the natural world shares with us everywhere we turn. Music may not be a luxury, but nor is it to be taken for granted; it will make our onward journey all the more pleasurable. We do not need to feel any burden of creativity, since we automatically form a vital part of the musical triangle (composer, performer, listener) just by being there, breathing in beautiful sounds and being open to gaining something revelatory from them.

Finally, we should resist judging our insides by other people's outsides – the impressive accomplishments of others tell us nothing about who *we* are, let alone our own potential to grow. The key is to become the best version of ourselves we possibly can. Mindful musicians and music lovers already have a head start in this regard, as I hope I have shown. Finding projects that seem bigger than ourselves – learning to play an instrument perhaps, beginning to compose music, or being enterprising in our discovery of new music – helps to give overarching shape and meaning to our lives. None of us is too old to have a plan, or too long in the tooth to take a fresh approach. Actually, I believe we all want a life that gets progressively better – a middle age that blossoms into an Indian summer and delivers us up at the autumn of our lives. But this will require us to search out our own pearls of wisdom and inner enlightenment, for the world is our musical oyster. Importantly, the enjoyment and satisfaction that springs from music should not be hemmed in by our perceived limitations, or indeed by the thoughtless dismissal of others. On the contrary, we should be focusing on what attributes we *do* have and *could* have; in short, the art of possibility.

BIBLIOGRAPHY & FURTHER READING

Crofton I. and Fraser D., eds, *A Dictionary of Musical Quotations* (Croom Helm, New York, 1985)
Dion, J., *The Art of Mindful Singing* (Leaping Hare Press, Brighton 2017)
Ford, A., *The Art of Mindful Silence* (Leaping Hare Press, Lewes, 2011)
Gladwell, M., *Outliers: The Story of Success* (Little, Brown & Co., Boston, 2008)
Gregory, D., *Shut Your Monkey: How to Control Your Inner Critic and Get More Done* (HOW Books, Cincinnati, 2016)
Jakubowski K., 'Dissecting an Earworm: Melodic Features and Song Popularity Predict Involuntary Musical Imagery', in *Psychology of Aesthetics, Creativity, and the Arts*, November 2016.
Khan, H. I., *The Mysticism of Sound and Music, The Sufi Teaching of Hazrat Inayat Khan* (Shambhala Dragon Editions, Boulder, 1996)
Ross, A., *The Rest Is Noise: Listening to the Twentieth Century* (Farrar, Straus & Giroux, New York, 2007)
Sacks, O., *Musicophilia: Tales of Music and the Brain* (Picador, London, 2008)
Şen, Emre, pianist, CD recording, sleeve: *The Gestalt Approach* (Lila Müzik, Istanbul, 2010)
Tanner, M., *The Mindful Pianist: Focus, Practise, Perform, Engage* (Faber Music, London, 2016)

WEBSITES

Alexander Technique: alexandertechnique.com
Chetham's International Piano Summer School: pianosummerschool.com
EPTA: epta-uk.org
Harry The Piano: harrythepiano.com
Jackdaws Education Trust: jackdaws.org.uk
John Nations, Juggler: blackburninternational.com
Mensa: mensa.org.uk
Pianist Magazine: pianistmagazine.com
Piano Dao (Andrew Eales): pianodao.com
Royal Society of Arts: thersa.org
Spartan Press (music publisher): spartanpress.co.uk
Paul Da Vinci (The Rubettes): pauldavinci.net

ABOUT THE AUTHOR

Mark Tanner is a concert pianist, composer and writer. He has broadcast on BBC Radio 3 and Classic FM, recorded extensively, and performed at London's Wigmore Hall and worldwide on cruise ships. Mark has a PhD and is a member of Mensa. Sixty volumes of his compositions have been published, and his book, *The Mindful Pianist*, is published by Faber. Mark embraces mindfulness in his creative life and in his teaching. Mark wishes to acknowledge Gillian Poznansky, for additional proof-reading and loving support.
marktanner.info Twitter: @MarkTannerPiano

INDEX

THE MINDFULNESS SERIES

The Art of Mindful Baking
Julia Ponsonby

The Art of Mindful Birdwatching
Claire Thompson

The Art of Mindful Gardening
Ark Redwood

The Art of Mindful Silence
Adam Ford

The Art of Mindful Singing
Jeremy Dion

The Art of Mindful Walking
Adam Ford

Einstein & the Art of Mindful Cycling
Ben Irvine

Galileo & the Art of Ageing Mindfully
Adam Ford

Happiness and How it Happens
The Happy Buddha

The Heart of Mindful Relationships
Maria Arpa

The Joy of Mindful Writing
Joy Kenward

The Mindful Art of Wild Swimming
Tessa Wardley

Mindful Thoughts for Cyclists
Nick Moore

Mindful Thoughts for Walkers
Adam Ford

Mindfulness & Compassion
The Happy Buddha

Mindfulness and Surfing
Sam Bleakley

Mindfulness & the Art of Drawing
Wendy Ann Greenhalgh

Mindfulness & the Art of Managing Anger
Mike Fisher

Mindfulness & the Art of Urban Living
Adam Ford

Mindfulness & the Journey of Bereavement
Peter Bridgewater

Mindfulness & the Natural World
Claire Thompson

Mindfulness at Work
Maria Arpa

Mindfulness for Black Dogs & Blue Days
Richard Gilpin

Mindfulness for Unravelling Anxiety
Richard Gilpin

The Mindfulness in Knitting
Rachael Matthews

Moments of Mindfulness

Naturally Mindful

Zen & the Path of Mindful Parenting
Clea Danaan

GEIRIAU GORFOLEDD A GALAR

Geiriau Gorfoledd a Galar

D. Geraint Lewis

Gomer

Llyfr Nia a Gwenllïan yw hwn.

Argraffwyd yn 2007 gan Wasg Gomer,
Llandysul, Ceredigion SA44 4JL

Adargraffwyd yn 2010

ISBN 978 1 84323 820 1

Dymuna'r cyhoeddwyr gydnabod cymorth
Adrannau Cyngor Llyfrau Cymru.

Argraffwyd a rhwymwyd yng Nghymru gan
Wasg Gomer, Llandysul, Ceredigion SA44 4JL

Cynnwys

Rhagair

Bydd pobl yn gofyn yn fynych am ddarnau addas i'w darllen mewn priodas ac angladd, darnau nad ydynt o reidrwydd yn benodol Gristnogol. Er chwilota dros gyfnod, methais â dod o hyd i unrhyw ffynhonnell amlwg yn Gymraeg. Pan ofynnais innau yn fy nhro i Wasg Gomer am lyfr o'r fath, a deall nad oedd un ar gael, dyna fan cychwyn y casgliad bach hwn.

Wrth chwilota, deuthum ar draws geiriau William Penn a ddyfynnir ar ddechrau'r gyfrol hon, 'Nid af heibio'r ffordd hon eto'; dyma'r geiriau sydd wedi gosod siâp i'r casgliad, ac sydd wrth wraidd pob dewis. Caru, priodi, magu teulu ac yna farwolaeth ei hun, cerrig milltir ydynt ar hyd ffordd bywyd.

Ond nid digon oedd casglu darnau i'w darllen ar achlysur priodas ac angladd yn unig. Yr oedd gan ein beirdd, ochr yn ochr â meddylwyr o wledydd eraill y byd, bethau i'w dweud am natur y ffordd hefyd ac am y teithiwr ei hun: sylwadau sy'n taflu goleuni ar begynau bywyd, y llon a'r lleddf, gwynfyd a galar – gwirioneddau am y natur ddynol o ba liw, o ba lun neu o ba gred bynnag.

Rwy'n gobeithio bod y ddalen gynnwys yn amlygu'r llwybr y dewisais ei ddilyn. I'r rheiny ohonoch sy'n penderfynu dilyn y ffordd bob cam, rwy'n hyderu y byddwch yn profi o leiaf rywfaint o'r wefr a'r boddhad a dderbyniais innau wrth ddarllen y deunydd yma drosodd a thro – ond rhaid i mi eich rhybuddio bod yma rai darnau sy'n ysgytwol o anghysurus. I'r rheiny ohonoch sy'n chwilio am ddarn ar gyfer achlysur arbennig, rwy'n gobeithio y dewch chi o hyd i rywbeth a fydd o gymorth i oleuo neu i gynhesu ychydig ar yr achlysur hwnnw.

D. Geraint Lewis
Llangwyryfon – Pasg 2007

Nid af heibio'r ffordd hon eto

Nid af heibio'r ffordd hon eto

Unwaith yn unig y tramwyaf ffordd bywyd. Felly, os gallaf amlygu caredigrwydd, neu wneuthur daioni i'm cyd-ddyn, gwnaf ef yn awr, canys nid af heibio'r ffordd hon eto.

William Penn

Croesi Traeth

Er rhoi troed ar lawer traeth,
Teithio a hwylio helaeth,
Nid yw yr holl grwydro hyn
Ragor na chasglu cregyn:
Ni adewir ar dywod
Hynt fy nhrem na phrint fy nhro'd.

Gwyn Evans

Y Dewis

Nid dy ddewis di yw pryd y byddi farw nac ym mha fodd. Dy ddewis di yw sut y byddi fyw.

Joan Baez

Duw biau edau bywyd
A'r hawl i fesur ei hyd.

Daniel Ddu o Geredigion

Dyn biau gadwyn bywyd
A'r hawl i'w thorri cyn pryd.

Einion Evans

Beth fu ddoe,
beth fory fydd

Bod

(Detholiad)

Beth fu ddoe, beth fory fydd,
Ba waeth sôn, wrth beth y sydd?
Bywyn Bod yw bod beunydd.

T. Gwynn Jones

Penillion o Omar Khayyâm

(Detholiad)

Fel llif mewn afon, ac fel gwynt ar draeth,
Dydd arall o derm f'einioes treiglo wnaeth;
Am ddau o ddyddiau ni ofidiaf fi,
Am ddydd i ddyfod, ac am ddydd a aeth.

John Morris-Jones

Ddoe, heddiw ac yfory

Heddiw yw'r yfory y bûm yn poeni amdano ddoe.

Anhysbys

Y Tragwyddol

Mae'r tragwyddol sydd ynot yn ymwybodol nad oes hualau amser i fywyd. Gŵyr mai dim ond cof heddiw yw ddoe, a breuddwyd heddiw yw yfory. Ac mae'r hyn a gân ac a fyfyria ynot yn preswylio o hyd yn yr ennyd gyntaf honno a wasgarodd y sêr hyd entrychion y nef.

Kahlil Gibran

Amser

(Addasiad o gerdd Almaeneg, 'Betrachtung der Zeit', gan Andreas Gryphius)

Nid fy eiddo i
yw'r blynyddoedd
a gipiodd amser
oddi arnaf.

Nid fy eiddo ychwaith
yw'r blynyddoedd
a ddaw imi.

Fy eiddo yw'r foment hon
a'r Hwn
a wnaeth
amser
a thragwyddoldeb.

D. Islwyn Edwards

Amser a Ddengys

Y mae amser i bob peth, ac amser i bob amcan dan y nefoedd;
Amser i eni, ac amser i farw; amser i blannu, ac amser i dynnu y peth a blannwyd;
Amser i ladd, ac amser i iacháu; amser i fwrw i lawr, ac amser i adeiladu;
Amser i wylo, ac amser i chwerthin; amser i alaru, ac amser i ddawnsio;
Amser i daflu cerrig ymaith, ac amser i gasglu cerrig ynghyd; amser i ymgofleidio, ac amser i ochel ymgofleidio;
Amser i geisio, ac amser i golli; amser i gadw, ac amser i fwrw ymaith;
Amser i rwygo, ac amser i wnïo; amser i dewi, ac amser i ddywedyd;
Amser i garu, ac amser i gasáu; amser i ryfel, ac amser i heddwch.

Llyfr y Pregethwr
(Pennod 3 1–8)

Amser

Ceisiwch amser i feddwl,
dyma ffynhonnell pob gallu.
Ceisiwch amser i chwarae,
dyma gyfrinach bod yn fythol ifanc.
Ceisiwch amser i ddarllen,
dyma ffynhonnell doethineb.
Ceisiwch amser i weddïo,
dyma'r grym mwyaf ar y Ddaear.
Ceisiwch amser i garu a chael eich caru,
dyma rodd fwyaf Duw.
Ceisiwch amser i fod yn gyfeillgar,
dyma lwybr llawenydd.
Ceisiwch amser i chwerthin,
dyma gân yr enaid.
Ceisiwch amser i roi,
dyma rydd fodlonrwydd.
Ceisiwch amser i weithio,
dyma bris llwyddiant.
Ceisiwch amser i fod yn garedig,
dyma'r allwedd i'r nefoedd.

Anhysbys

Treigl Amser

Fel y rhed yr haul i'r hwyr,
Fel y treulia'r gannwyll gŵyr,
Fel y syrthia'r rhosyn gwyn,
Fel y diffydd tarth ar lyn.

Ni cheir gweled mwy o'n hôl,
Nag ôl neidr ar y ddôl,
Neu ôl llong aeth dros y tonnau,
Neu ôl saeth mewn awyr denau.

Y Ficer Prichard

Pa beth yw Amser?

Mae amser
yn rhy araf
        i'r rhai sy'n aros,
yn rhy fuan
        i'r rhai sy'n ofni,
yn rhy hir
        i'r rhai sy'n galaru,
yn rhy fyr
        i'r rhai sy'n llawenhau,
ond i'r rhai sy'n caru,
mae amser yn Dragywydd.

Henry Van Dyke

A hyn hefyd a â heibio

Y Fodrwy

Bu'r Brenin Solomon yn ymgynghori â'i wŷr doeth. Gofynnodd iddynt am rywbeth a fyddai'n ei lonni pan fyddai'n drist, ond a fyddai'n peri iddo bwyllo pan fyddai'n llawen. Ymhen amser, dychwelasant a rhoddi iddo fodrwy ac arni'r geiriau:

A hyn hefyd a â heibio.

Anhysbys

Graffiti yn Pompeii

Llynca'r môr yr haul mawr melyn;
Lleuad lawn sy'n edwi wedyn;
Corwynt ddoe dry'n awel dyner:
Does dim byd yn para llawer.

Myrddin ap Dafydd

Penillion o Omar Khayyâm

(Detholiad)

Y Meistr ei Hun a fu'n cymysgu'n clai,
A pham y myn ddifetha'r cyfryw rai?
Od ydyw'r llestr yn hardd, paham y'i torrir?
Ac onid ydyw'n hardd, ar bwy mae'r bai?

Yn wir, rhyw ddernyn gwyddbwyll ydyw dyn,
Tynged yn chware â hwnnw 'i chware 'i hun;
Ein symud ar glawr Bywyd, ôl a blaen,
A'n dodi 'mlwch yr Angau, un ac un.

A chan mai gwir y gair, pa les yw dwyn,
Oherwydd dy drabluddiau, och a chŵyn?
Dygymydd di â'th dynged – ni thry'r Pin*
I newid un llythyren er dy fwyn.

Bydd lawen yn dy fywyd, na fydd brudd;
A meithrin farn yn lle'r ffolineb sydd;
A chan nad ydyw'r byd i gyd ond diddim,
Cyfrif nad wyt ond diddim, a bydd rydd!

John Morris-Jones

* y pin sy'n ysgrifennu ein tynged.

Dychwelyd

Ni all terfysgoedd daear byth gyffroi
Distawrwydd nef; ni sigla lleisiau'r llawr
Rymuster y tangnefedd sydd yn toi
Diddim diarcholl yr ehangder mawr;
Ac ni all holl drybestod dyn a byd
Darfu'r tawelwch nac amharu dim
Ar dreigl a thro'r pellterau sydd o hyd
Yn gwneuthur gosteg â'u chwyrnellu chwim.
Ac am nad ydyw'n byw ar hyd y daith
O gri ein geni hyd ein holaf gŵyn
Yn ddim ond crych dros dro neu gysgod craith
Ar lyfnder esmwyth y mudandod mwyn,
Ni wnawn, wrth ffoi am byth o'n ffwdan ffôl,
Ond llithro i'r llonyddwch mawr yn ôl.

T. H. Parry-Williams

Dyfod

Dywedwyd na wnawn ni, feidrol fodau,
Wrth ffoi, yn y diwedd un, o'n ffwdan ffôl
Ond llithro i'r llonyddwch mawr yn ôl.

Ond, wedyn,
Pam a sut y daethom yma –
Os o ryw lonyddwch mawr –
Yn y lle cynta'?

Oni ellir, i'r gwrthwyneb hefyd, honni
Ei bod hi'r un mor debygol fod yna
Yn y bydysawd diorffwys
Dragwyddol drybestod, cyffroadau,
Nerthoedd symudadwy,
Galluoedd egr, ffrwydriadau ysgethrin,
A thymhestloedd cosmig;
Rhyw rym o rywle, rhyw egni o'r tu hwnt inni
Anorchfygol, diamodol, parhaol o fodoli?

Gwyn Thomas

Pe Cawn

Pe cawn
Yn waddol fore a nawn,
A dydd hirfelyn,
A chainc ar delyn,
A hinon haf ar dwyn,
A byd di-gur di-gŵyn:
Pa les
Dihoeni yn y tes,
A blino'n llwyr
Am na ddôi Hwyr?
Heb wyll, heb wawr;
Heb nos, heb sêr;
Heb gystudd mawr,
Heb acen bêr;
Ac ni fai nef yn nef yn wir
Pe nef ond dydd o olau hir.

John Dyfnallt Owen

Mewn Llythyr

Megis yn eithaf grym y storm y mae
Ennyd o osteg yn fyddardod mawr,
Neu'r lleuad rhwng cymylau fel petae
Yn fil disgleiriach na goleuni gwawr;
Megis y cwyd yr eog yn ei bryd
Yn uwch ei naid po ddyfna'r pwll islaw,
A dilyn drwy greigleoedd garwa'r rhyd
Ei siwrne ordeiniedig i'w phen draw;
Megis ar feysydd cad y gwelwyd holl
Eithafion dyn, ei orau a'i waethaf dall,
Mae heth a hindda y blynyddoedd coll
Yng nghiliau'r co'n dwysáu y naill y llall.
Nid oes na gwên na gwae pan ballo'r nwyd,
Na du na gwyn yn y cyffredin llwyd.

Dic Jones

Yr Efengyl yn ôl Rusty James

(Detholiad)

Nid oes ryddid yn y byd
yr wyf innau'n ei adnabod
nad yw'n troi'n gaethiwed clyd
wrth im synfyfyrio ormod
ar ei odidowgrwydd agos
(ces fy ngeni'n groes i'r graen):
pan fydd Duw yn sibrwd "Aros",
dyna adeg symud 'mlaen.

Emyr Lewis

Beth ydyw bywyd?

Geiriau Crowfoot ar ei wely angau

Beth ydyw bywyd?
Fflachiad y gwyfyn drwy'r gwyll,
Anadl yr ychen yn y bore bach,
Y cysgod chwim sy'n rhedeg drwy'r glaswellt
i ymgolli'n y machlud.

Arfon Huws

Pa Beth yw Dyn?

Beth yw byw? Cael neuadd fawr
Rhwng cyfyng furiau.
Beth yw adnabod? Cael un gwraidd
Dan y canghennau.

Beth yw credu? Gwarchod tref
Nes dyfod derbyn.
Beth yw maddau? Cael ffordd trwy'r drain
At ochr hen elyn.

Beth yw canu? Cael o'r creu
Ei hen athrylith.
Beth yw gweithio ond gwneud cân
O'r coed a'r gwenith?

Beth yw trefnu teyrnas? Crefft
Sydd eto'n cropian.
A'i harfogi? Rhoi'r cyllyll
yn llaw'r baban.

Beth yw bod yn genedl? Dawn
Yn nwfn y galon.
Beth yw gwladgarwch? Cadw tŷ
Mewn cwmwl tystion.

Beth yw'r byd i'r nerthoedd mawr?
Cylch yn treiglo.
Beth yw'r byd i blant y llawr?
Crud yn siglo

Waldo Williams

Os

Os gelli gadw'th ben a phawb o'th gwmpas
Yn colli eu pennau'n llwyr a'th feio di,
Os cedwi ffydd a phawb yn amau'th bwrpas
A rhoi ystyriaeth deg i'w hamheuon ri;
Os gelli ddisgwyl heb flino gwneuthur hynny,
Neu oddef cam heb dalu cam yn ôl,
Ac er dy gasáu – parhau i garu,
Heb osgo un difai'n 'sgoi siarad ffôl.

Os gelli synfyfyrio ac ymateb
Os gelli feddwl heb wneud hynny'n nod;
Os gelli gwrdd â llwyddiant a thrychineb
A rhoi i'r twyllwyr hyn 'run faint o glod;
Os gelli oddef clywed amryw ddynion
Yn troi dy wir i dwyllo gwirion ŵr,
A gweled llafur d'oes yn mynd yn deilchion,
A phigo'r darnau i fyny heb ddim stŵr.

Os gelli gynnull dy holl fydol bethau
A'u mentro oll ar ryw hap-chware chwim,
A cholli'r cyfan, yna dechrau o'r dechrau
Heb yngan gair am loes a bod heb ddim;
Os gelli yrru calon, nerf a gewyn
I wneud dy waith ar ôl eu darfod hwy,
A dal i fynd pan nad oes gennyt fymryn
Ond grym ewyllys dd'wed 'Dal ati'n hwy'.

Os gelli fod mewn torf yn lân dy ddwylo,
Neu feddu golud byd a chofio'r tlawd,
Os na all gelyn na hoff gâr dy glwyfo,
Os perchi di bob dyn, waeth beth fo'i ffawd;
Os gelli lenwi'r didosturiol funud
Â thrigain eiliad o weithredu gras,
Eiddot ti yw'r ddaear a'i holl olud,
A pheth sy'n fwy – fe fyddi'n ddyn, fy ngwas!

Owen R. Hughes
yn seiliedig ar gerdd Rudyard Kipling

Desiderata

Dos yn ddedwydd ymhlith y dwndwr a'r ffrwst,
a chofia'r heddwch a geir mewn tawelwch.
Hyd eithaf dy allu, a heb ildio,
bydd yn gyfaill i bob enaid byw.
Llefara dy wirionedd yn dawel a chlir;
Rho glust i eraill,
Hyd yn oed y diflas a'r dywedwst;
Mae gan bob un ei stori.

Ceisia osgoi'r swnllyd a'r swagrog,
Fe flinant dy ysbryd.
Os bydd i ti gymharu dy hun ag eraill
Fe all yr ei di'n falch a chwerw;
Bydd wastad rai yn fwy na thi – a rhai yn llai;
Mwynha dy lwyddiant law yn llaw â gobaith.

Cymer ddiddordeb yn dy yrfa, waeth pa mor ddistadl;
y mae'n eiddo i ti ynghanol pob newid a ddaw i'th ran.
Bydd ochelgar ym myd dy fusnes;
Mae'r byd yn llawn o dwyll.
Ond na foed i hynny dy ddallu i'r daioni sydd;
Bydd llawer yn ymgyrraedd at ddelfryd
Ac mae bywyd yn llawn o arwriaeth.

Ti wyt ti. Bydd felly.
Yn enwedig, paid cogio caru.
Paid ychwaith ag wfftio serch;
Yn y crindir digalon
Y mae mor feunyddiol â'r borfa las.

Rho glust garedig i gyngor doeth profiad,
Gan ildio'n rasol bethau bachgennaidd.
Maga gryfder ysbryd yn gysgod rhag cawod chwith,
Ond paid â drysu gan ddrwgfeddyliau du.
Ffrwyth blinder ac unigrwydd yw llawer gofid.
Oddieithr disgyblaeth iach,
Bydd yn fwyn â thi dy hun.

Rwyt blentyn y bydysawd,
Yn gymaint â'r coed a'r sêr.
Mae gennyt hawl i fod yma.
Waeth beth a weli ac a feddyli di,
Mae'r bydysawd yn ymagor fel y dylai.

Bydd yn ddedwydd yn Nuw, felly,
Pa beth bynnag fo Duw i ti,
A pha beth bynnag dy ymdrech a'th uchelgais
Yn y dadwrdd dryslyd, boed i'th enaid gael hedd.

Er gwaetha pob ffug, pob trymder, pob breuddwyd
  chwâl
Byd bendigedig yw hwn.
Anela am hapusrwydd
A bydd lawen.

addas. Bethan Mair
yn seiliedig ar waith Max Ehrmann

Atgno

Gresyn im esgeuluso mor ddi-hid
  Groniclo'r cyffroadau gynt a gawn
Ar hwyr a bore mewn perlewyg prid,
  Ac ym myfyrdod moethus hir brynhawn,
Gan dybied y doent eilwaith yn eu tro
  Ar wyliau coch eu calendr tua thref,
A dwyn hen gynyrfiadau er cyn co'
  Yng ngwib y gwyntoedd o gilfachau'r nef;
Nes canfod, wrth im ddisgwyl mwy na mwy,
  Pan dreiglo dydd a phan fo nos yn cau,
Nad oes ond unwaith prin i'w dyfod hwy,
  Nad ydyw hoen eu haros yn parhau,
Ac na ddaw dim yn ôl o'r pedwar gwynt –
Dim ond rhyw frithgo' am ryw gyffro gynt.

T. H. Parry-Williams

Yr Einioes

(Detholiad)

Ymholaf pa ddirgelwch a fu'n rhoi
Ynof yr egni hwn nad oes un grym
A'i ceidw'n gaeth. Pa angerdd sy'n cyffroi
Pŵer a'm gyr nad oes a'i rhwystra ddim?
Pan ddeffry'r nwyd anfarwol yn y fron
A'r hen wrthryfel sydd yng nghuro'r gwaed,
Nid oes a saif ar lwybr yr antur hon
Ac nid oes atal ar garlamu'r traed.
Pa beth yw'r daith ai hynt o'r pridd i'r pridd
A gorffwys eto'n isel yn y clai –
Ennyd i lithro ar lifeiriant sydd
Yn mynd i'w dragwyddoldeb yn ddi-drai?
Cael egwyl fach rhwng dau ddistawrwydd mawr
I brofi o sylwedd Bywyd ar y llawr?

J. M. Edwards

Rheswm ac Angerdd

Ar fordaith bywyd eich rheswm a'ch angerdd yw llyw a hwyliau yr enaid.

Pe torrai'r llyw a'r hwyliau, crwydro'n ddigyfeiriad neu din-droi ynghanol y môr fyddai eich rhan.

Mae rheswm, ar ei ben ei hun, yn rym sy'n caethiwo, ac angerdd dilyffethair yn fflam ysol sy'n difa ei hun.

Boed i'ch enaid glodfori eich rheswm yn angerddol hyd oni chano; a boed i'ch enaid lywio eich angerdd â rheswm fel y byddo fyw drwy atgyfodi'n feunyddiol, a chodi megis ffenics o'i ludw ei hun.

Kahlil Gibran

Rhyfeddod mewn dwy galon

Gwreiddiau

(Detholiad)

Unwaith, amser maith a mwy yn ôl,
i fyd yn llawn dyfodol,
fe aned mewn dwy fynwes
un wên fach –
a hynny ar hap.

A heb yn wybod
plannwyd hedyn
o ryfeddod
mewn dwy galon.

Daeth yn sydyn
mas o ddim
i fwrw'i wreiddyn.

Ac un diwrnod,
heb ofyn,
daeth blaguryn

yn fory i gyd . . .

Mererid Hopwood

Aelwyd

Gan ddau y lluniwyd ei chlyd barwydydd,
Trwsiad eu cariad fu'n harddu'r ceyrydd;
Arni lluniem fin hwyr ein llawenydd,
A rhannu galar a chur ein gilydd;
Rhag gwae'r storm, rhag gwres y dydd – awn bob tro
I chwilio am yr 'echel lonydd'.

T. Llew Jones

I'm Hanwylyd

Trwy ddirgel ffyrdd
Fe ddaethost ti
Fel iâr fach yr haf
I'm bywyd i.

Yn sgil yr awel
A'n chwythodd ynghyd
Daeth newydd lawenydd
I'n dau fyd.

Fel gwres Gorffennaf
Ar stodau'r gwair
Yw sensitifrwydd
Y deall di-air.

'Does rwymyn anwylach
Mewn unrhyw stad
Na hen naturioldeb
Cefn gwlad.

Dy wyneb a'th gorff
Yn dlws fel y maent
Ac i'th berson yr harddwch
Sy'n ddyfnach na phaent.

Curiad calon
Yn dy eiriau serch
Ac agos gynhesrwydd
Y ddethol ferch.

A phwy yn wir
Drwy'r cread crwn
A allai wrthsefyll
Y cariad hwn?

* * *

Ni fedraf esbonio dyfnder fy serch
Atat ti, fy nigymar ferch.

Mae tinc dy lais a'th lygaid glas,
Dy wyneb a'th gorff yn peri ias.

Ond mae rhywbeth mwy na'th brydferthwch di
Yn dal i rwydo fy nghalon i.

Cadwyn cyd-ddeall sy rhyngom ein dau
A'r cyntaf gynhesrwydd yn mynnu parhau.

'Rwy'n dy garu'n fwy nag un ferch yn y byd,
Ni alla' i ragor, a dyna i gyd.

John Roderick Rees

Grym Cariad

Pan eilw Cariad, dilyna ef, er garwed a serth ei ffyrdd.
A phan gofleidia di â'i adenydd, anwesa ef,
Er i frath y cledd sy' ynghudd yn ei blu dy glwyfo.
A phan siarado, cred ynddo,
Er i'w lais chwalu dy freuddwydion, fel y difa'r gogledd-wynt y gerddi.
Oherwydd, fel y bydd Cariad yn dy goroni, bydd hefyd yn dy groeshoelio.
Fel y dyhea am dy dyfiant, bydd hefyd yn dy docio,
Fel yr esgyn i'th ganghennau uchaf ac anwesu'r mân frigau bregus sy'n crynu yn yr haul,
Felly y disgynna i'th wreiddiau a'u hysgwyd o'u gafael yn y pridd.

Kahlil Gibran

Cariad

Ynot ti mae tân,
oglau Awst, tir glân
a'r gawod gân ar goed y gwanwyn.

Ynot ti mae ton,
gŵyl yn y galon,
unigolion yn wyn i'w gilydd.

Ynot ti mae taw
y llais, dim ond llaw
yn rhwyfo'r llaw ar fôr y lleuad.

Ynot ti mae taith
y tu hwnt i iaith
a hen, hen obaith hŷn na nabod.

Myrddin ap Dafydd

Hanner

Mae gan berson cyflawn bedair coes,
deugain o fysedd (gan gynnwys y traed),
dau ben, dau ymennydd i reoli gwaith
ffatrïoedd y mêr yn labordai'r gwaed
ac mae hiraeth ofnadwy yn llenwi'r rhai
sy'n sengl, ond heb hanner eu henaid.

Priodas yw dinas yr haneri coll
sy'n chwilio ymhlith y ffracsiynau di-ri'
am fathemateg a all asio dau
a'u lluosogi i fod yn dri,
gan ddymchwel holl onglau bod ar wahân
ac ailosod y 'rheiny' yn rhan o'r 'ni'.

Pob clod i gyfanrwydd y bodau llawn
ac aml-lygeidiog sy'n mynd yn hen
wrth gau ar ei gilydd fel llyfrau trwm,
eu cloriau'n cenhedlu clasuron ein llên
a dalennau eu caru fel glöyn byw
yn llosgi mewn cusan, yn llachar mewn gwên.

Gwyneth Lewis

Mi Gerddaf Gyda Thi

Mi gerddaf gyda thi dros lwybrau maith,
A blodau, cân a breuddwyd ar ein taith;
I'th lygaid syllaf i a dal dy law:
Mi gerddaf gyda thi, beth bynnag ddaw.

Mi gerddaf gyda thi pan fydd y lloer
Fel llusern yn y nen ar noson oer.
Addawaf i ti 'nghalon i yn llwyr:
Mi gerddaf gyda thi drwy oriau'r hwyr.

Mi gerddaf gyda thi drwy weddill f'oes,
Pan fydd yr haul ar fryn, neu'r dyddiau'n groes;
A phan ddaw'r alwad draw, pwy ŵyr pa awr,
Mi gerddaf gyda thi i'r freuddwyd fawr.

Anhysbys

Y Daith

(Detholiad)

Yn oer, yn unig, ar siwrne anodd,
Yn eira'r galar hyhi a'm gwelodd,
Yng nghiliau'r hiraeth fy nghlwy a irodd,
Yn waglaw oeddwn, fe'm hymgeleddodd,
Ei hanwes a'm cynhesodd, – a thyner
Oedd ei llaw, ei hyder a'm hailddilladodd.

Idris Reynolds

Llwy garu

Er mor dyner fu'r cerfiad – yr addurn
sy'n rhwydd ei ddirywiad,
nid o'r cŵyr y daw'r cariad,
yn y pren y mae'r parhad.

Emyr Lewis

Haelioni Cariad

Rhoi a wna Cariad, nid cymryd,
Trystio a chredu, nid hau annedwyddyd,
Rhoi nawdd amyneddgar gan rannu yn hygar
Pob siom a llawenydd,
Ddoe, heddiw, ie! Beunydd.

Â'i awen anniwall bydd Cariad yn deall.
Mae'n gryf. Daw o'r galon.
Mae'n gysur. Mae'n gyson.
Ac i ddau gâr ei gilydd
Mae'n gwlwm tragywydd.

Anhysbys
addas. Desmond Healy

Priodas

(Addasiad o anerchiad priodas llwyth yr Apache.)

Boed i chwi egni newydd
Liw dydd yng ngwres yr haul,
A thyner wawl y lleuad
Liw nos i fwrw'r draul,
A golched cynnes gawod law
I ffwrdd eich gofid a phob braw.

Chwythed awelon ysgafn
I adnewyddu'ch nerth,
Ac na foed i chwi lithro
Lle byddo'r llwybrau'n serth.
Boed i chwi'n ysgafn droedio'r byd
Gan roi i'r ddaear barch o hyd.

Corwynt na thywydd garw
Eich taro mwy ni all
Tra bo'ch yng nghwmni'ch gilydd
Yn gysgod naill i'r llall,
A phan fo llwydrew'n cwympo'r mes
Fe fydd y naill i'r llall yn wres.

Dwy galon, un dyhead,
Dau dafod ond un iaith,
Dwy raff yn cydio'n ddolen,
Dau enaid ond un daith.
Fe fydd cwmnïaeth yn parhau,
Nid oes unigrwydd lle bo dau.

Rhagoch i'ch pabell bellach
I gadw tân ynghynn,
Y drws i bawb ar agor
A'r holl linynnau'n dynn.
Doed eich breuddwydion oll yn wir,
Boed fyr eich llid a'ch cof yn hir.

Dic Jones

Allwedd Cariad

Allwedd cariad yw deall . . .
y gallu i ddirnad nid yn unig y geiriau
ond yr ystumiau mud
a'r arwyddion bychain sydd mor huawdl.

Allwedd cariad yw maddeuant . . .
derbyn beiau eich gilydd a'u maddau
heb eu diystyru, ond gan gofio'r
hyn a ddysgwyd oddi wrthynt.

Allwedd cariad yw rhannu . . .
wynebu hawddfyd ac adfyd gyda'ch gilydd,
a goresgyn anawsterau a cheisio ffyrdd
i ddyfnhau eich llawenydd.

Allwedd cariad yw rhoi . . .
heb ddisgwyl derbyn
y wên gynnil, gynnes
yr ildio a'r ymdrechu.

Allwedd cariad yw parch . . .
sylweddoli eich bod yn ddau unigolyn â syniadau gwahanol,
sylweddoli nad ydych yn berchennog, y naill ar y llall
ond eich bod yn rhannu'r ymdeimlad o berthyn,
yn rhannu rhwymyn cudd.

Mae allwedd cariad o'n mewn ni i gyd . . .
amser ac amynedd all ddatgloi'r drws sy'n arwain i'w gynteddau;
mae'n hawlio ymdrech oes gan ddeuddyn ond telir ar ei ganfed am ymroddiad –

a dyna allwedd cariad.

Anhysbys

Cwlwm Serch

Nid cadwynau sy'n clymu priodas ond edafedd. Cannoedd o fân linynnau yn pwytho dau ynghyd dros y blynyddoedd. Dyma rydd barhad i briodas.

Simone Signoret

Y Gwir Ddedwyddwch

Ymhlith pethau cyffredin bywyd y cenfydd dyn wir ddedwyddwch. Nid golud, dysg, athrylith nac awdurdod yw ffynhonnell gwir ddedwyddwch. Ond yn hytrach iechyd, cyfeillgarwch, cartref cariadus, clywed lleisiau plant, teimlo heulwen haf: y rhain, bendithion cyffredin bywyd, a rydd wir ddedwyddwch.

Anhysbys

Cymer ddarn o glai

Cymer ddarn o glai a'i wlychu a'i fowldio.
Yn ddelw ohonof i a delw ohonot ti.
Cymer hwy eilwaith, eu chwalu, eu malu,
Ac wedi eu gwlychu, ail-lunio
Delw ohonof i a delw ohonot ti.
Bellach, bydd yn fy nghlai i beth ohonot ti
Ac yn dy glai di beth ohonof fi,
Ac ni ellir byth eu gwahanu.
Yn fyw, cysgwn o dan yr un cwrlid;
Yn farw, cawn orwedd ynghyd.

Kuan Tao-Sheng

Gwersi Bywyd

Ymhen tipyn
Fe ddysgi'r gwahaniaeth
Rhwng cydio llaw
A chaethiwo enaid.
Fe ddysgi nad pwyso wna cariad
Ond cynnal.
Fe ddoi di i dderbyn dy fethiannau
Â gras oedolyn
Nid â galar plentyn.

Penderfyni sefydlu dy lwybrau ar heddiw
Gan fod tir yfory
Yn dir rhy simsan.
Fe roi di help llaw i arall blannu gardd
Yn lle disgwyl iddo gynnig iti flodau.
Daw sicrwydd fod Duw wedi rhoi iti'r
Nerth i ddal ati,
A bod iti wir werth.

Anhysbys

Cyngor

Boed dy gariad yn drech na'th ddicter.
Dysg ddoethineb cyfaddawdu, canys gwell yw plygu ychydig na thorri.
Cred y gorau, nid y gwaethaf. Bydd ymarweddiad pobl yn ddrych o'th farn amdanynt.
Cofia mai cyfeillgarwch diledryw yw sylfaen pob perthynas a bâr.
Estyn i'th briod yr hynawsedd a'r cymwynasgarwch a roddi i'th gyfeillion.
Dysg hyn oll i'th blant a phlant dy blant.

seiliedig ar gyngor Jane Wells

Bendith Indiaid America

Ni theimlwch mwyach y glaw
Gan y byddwch yn gysgod y naill i'r llall.
Ni theimlwch yr oerfel,
Gan y bydd y naill yn cynhesu'r llall.
Ni theimlwch unigrwydd
Gan y byddwch yn gwmni i'ch gilydd.
Yn awr yr ydych yn ddeuddyn
ond y mae tri bywyd o'ch blaen: ei fywyd ef, ei bywyd hi a'ch bywyd gyda'ch gilydd.

Ewch yn awr i'ch cartref
er mwyn treulio dyddiau eich bywyd ynghyd.
Boed i chwi harddwch yn gymar ar eich taith,
ac ar hyd y blynyddoedd boed dedwyddwch yn gwmni i chwi
nes cyrraedd y man lle mae'r afon a'r haul yn dod yn un.
A boed dyddiau da a maith i chwi ar y ddaear hon.

Parchwch eich gilydd
a pharchwch eich hunain
ac atgoffwch eich gilydd yn aml o'r hyn a'ch tynnodd ynghyd.
Yn anad dim cofiwch fod yn dyner, yn dirion, ac yn garedig i'ch gilydd.
Pan ddaw siomedigaethau, anawsterau ac ofn i'ch blino –
Fel a ddaw i bawb yn eu tro –
Cofiwch ganolbwyntio ar yr hyn sy'n dda rhyngoch, nid yn unig ar yr hyn sydd o'i le.
Dyma'r ffordd i oresgyn y stormydd a ddaw i'ch bywyd,
Pan fydd cymylau yn cuddio wyneb yr haul.

Anhysbys

Fy maban gwyn

I'm Mab

Daethost, ac fe'n gwnaethost yn un, rhag i'r gwynt brwysg ein nithio,
a thynhau y rhwymyn rhwng dau a oedd eisoes yn dynn:
ti yw'r haul sy'n meirioli'r heth, ti yw'r un sydd yn rhithio
pob gofid yn gerdd, ac fe gedwi ein hangerdd ynghýn.

Ie, ti yw'r cyfannwr tawel, ti yw'r chwa a chwery
â'r ddwyfflam gam, gan eu hasio yn unfflam hir;
ti yw bwa'r glaw wedi'r gawod, y bont rhwng dau bentir a bery
i'n huno'n gynghanedd, y gromen rhwng deupen o dir.

Ti yw'r dafn rhwng ein deulafn a'n deil, y gwlithyn a'n hunodd,
nes i welltyn gysylltu â gwelltyn yn ddiwahân.
Ein tair einioes nid ŷnt ar wahân: ti yw'r un a'u cyfunodd,
ti yw'r geiriau, a ninnau'r cyweiriau, ond un yw ein cân;

a phan fo dieithrwch rhyngom, a'n distawrwydd yn ddistawrwydd dieiriau
byddi'n chwalu'r gwahanfur â gwên, ac yn datod yr holl lyffetheiriau.

Alan Llwyd

Eirlys

Lliwiodd y moroedd dy lygaid
Cusanodd y rhosyn dy rudd,
Nentydd y mynydd a luniodd
Brydferthwch dy chwerthin cudd.

Ystwythder dy freichiau bychain,
A'r nerth sy'n dy fysedd di,
A miwsig dy iaith ddi-eiriau
Sy'n fythol ryfeddod i mi.

Gwynfil Rees

Mil Harddach Wyt

Mil harddach wyt na'r rhosyn gwyn,
Na'r rhosyn coch ar ael y bryn,
Na'r alarch balch yn nofio'r llyn,
Fy maban bach.

Mwy swynol yw dy chwerthin mwyn
Na chân y fronfraith yn y llwyn,
Na murmur môr o ben y twyn,
Fy maban bach.

Mwy annwyl wyt na'r oenig gwyn,
Na'r blodau tlws ar ochrau'r bryn,
Na dawnsio heulwen ar y llyn,
Fy maban bach.

Mil gwell gen i nag aur y byd,
Yw gweld dy wenau yn dy grud,
Fy ffortiwn wyt, a gwyn fy myd,
Fy maban bach.

Traddodiadol

Yn Nheyrnas Diniweidrwydd

(Detholiad)

Yn nheyrnas diniweidrwydd –
    Gwyn fyd pob plentyn bach
Sy'n berchen llygaid llawen
    A phâr o fochau iach!
Yn nheyrnas diniweidrwydd –
    Gwae hwnnw, wrth y pyrth:
Rhy hen i brofi'r syndod,
    Rhy gall i weld y wyrth!

Rhydwen Williams

Cyw a fegir yn Uffern,
yn Uffern y myn fod

Y plentyn sy'n cael ei farnu
A ddysg i gollfarnu.

Y plentyn sy'n cael ei orthrymu
A ddysg i ymladd.

Y plentyn sy'n cael ei wawdio
A ddysg swildod.

Y plentyn sy'n cael ei gywilyddio
A ddysg euogrwydd.

Y plentyn sy'n derbyn goddefgarwch
A ddysg amynedd.

Y plentyn sy'n derbyn anogaeth
A ddysg hyder.

Y plentyn sy'n derbyn canmoliaeth
A ddysg i werthfawrogi eraill.

Y plentyn sy'n cael ei drin yn deg
A ddysg gyfiawnder.

Y plentyn sy'n byw'n ddiogel
A ddysg i ymddiried.

Y plentyn sy'n cael ei ganmol
A ddysg hunan-barch.

Y plant sy'n cael eu derbyn ac sy'n profi
  cyfeillgarwch
A ddysg sut i ganfod cariad yn y byd.

Anhysbys

A fager ymysg cŵn a ddysg i gyfarth a chnoi.

Dadeni

(Detholiad)

D'eni heno yw 'nadeni innau
i stori gariad ac ystyr geiriau
fel 'mam' a 'dad' tu hwnt i 'mhrofiadau,
a bywyd eilwaith mewn byd o olau.
Yn yr heddiw llawn lliwiau, ar unwaith
af ar y daith i'th yfory dithau.

Curaf yn eiddgar – mae drysau 'nghariad
yn dal i agor yng nglas dy lygad.
Rwy'n newydd sbon, a thi yw'r esboniad
yn magu miri – dyma gymeriad!
Watwarwr siŵr dy siarad, dy un wên
yn chwarae'r awen, yw'r ail-ddechreuad.

Mererid Hopwood

Cysur

Rhyw un awr mor werthfawr yw,
awr hud o gysur ydyw,
awr i dad gael stori'r dydd
yn bennod ar obennydd;
ei geiriau'n bwyllog ara'
cyn chwifio'i dwylo nos da.

Ni ŵyr hon fod rhieni
trwy'r nos yn ei haros hi.
Amdani, cael mam dyner
a saif, fel y saif y sêr,
wastad i wylio drosti,
a chael tad i'w chlywed hi.
Yna, ei chael yn groeniach,
yn wyneb i'r bore bach;
dod gan chwifio dwylo'r dydd,
yn fore llawn lleferydd.
Rhoi, o'r nos, y bore i ni,
A thrannoeth, y wawr inni.

Tudur Dylan Jones

Cyfaill

Dau wyneb yn tebygu,
Dwy law yn cydio'n dynn,
Y naill ar drothwy bywyd
A'r llall â'i wallt yn wyn.

Ac wrth i un heneiddio
A'r llall i dyfu'n iau
Mae bwlch o ddwy genhedlaeth
Rhwng taid a'i ŵyr yn cau.

Ken Griffiths

Y cythraul diwyneb

Codi'r Caead

(Detholiad)

Aros am funud, 'rhen gyfaill,
Ista am funud ar y sêt.
Lle buost ti neithiwr yn crwydro?
Dywed wrtha i rŵan, 'rhen fêt.

Fuost ti'n crymanu tua Gwynedd 'na neithiwr?
Geriatrics dosbarth canol neu grach?
Neu adyn o'r hen wêr dosbarth gweithiol
Blannodd dwca yng ngwddf plentyn bach?

Fuost ti'n sblatro cnawd hyd yr Wyddfa?
Neu'n chwydu i 'sgyfaint ddŵr hallt?
Neu'n hogi dy gleddyf wrth ripio
Iraniad o'i geilliau i'w wallt?

Fuost ti draw yng Nghrosmaglen neithiwr
Yn mycspredio milwyr yn rhes?
'Nest ti gadw'r ddysgl yn wastad?
Alwest ti yng ngharchar y Maze?

Pwy wyt ti, y cythraul diwyneb,
A'th fach sgota yn plycio y cnawd?
Wrth dy wylio yn hacio teuluoedd
A bwtshera cig ysig fy mrawd.

Tyrd yma a dywed dy stori
Ond mwyach ni chei gen i barch,
Hen fastard dan-din wyt ti, angau.
Tyrd, eistedd ar gaead fy arch.

Derec Tomos

Credo in un Deo Crudel

Unawd Iago allan o opera Verdi 'Othello'

Credaf yn Nuw, y creulon
a'm creodd ar ei ddelw ei hun
ac mewn casineb rwy'n ei gydnabod.
O ryw hedyn erchyll
neu atom ffiaidd y'm cenhedlwyd.
Yr wyf gythraul – yr wyf ddyn –
a theimlaf ynof y llysnafedd cyntefig.
Yn wir, dyma fy nhystiolaeth.
Credaf â'm holl galon,
fel y weddw ieuanc wrth yr allor,
pa ffieidd-dra bynnag a feddaf
neu a ddaw ohonof,
gan Ffawd y'i tyngwyd i'm rhan.
Credaf nad yw dyn gonest
ond actor gwael ei wedd:
celwydd yw popeth yn ei gylch;
dagrau, cusanau, ei drem,
aberthau ac anrhydedd.
Credaf mai tegan
Ffawd anghyfiawn ydyw dyn
o eginyn y crud
hyd at bryf y bedd.
Ac wedi'r holl wawdio hyn, angau.
Ac yna? Ac yna?
Dim oll.
Breuddwyd gwrach yw'r Nef.

Boito

Eloï, Eloï, lema sabachthani

Eloï, Eloï, lema sabachthani

Fy Nuw, fy Nuw paham y'm gadewaist?

Marc 15[34]

A'r nos amdanaf yn cau

Ymwacâd

Fe ddaw'r adeg i tithau rywdro roddi hwrdd
I'th lu trugareddau, a'u lluchio hwy dros y bwrdd,

Gan ymlanhau o'r holl betheuach a fu
Yn ymgasglu o'th fewn fel ceriach yn hel mewn tŷ.

Fe deflir y ddysg sy'n haen ar d'ymennydd fel cen,
Heb sôn am yr holl anialwch sydd yn dy ben.

Bydd y sbonc a fu'n sionci dy galon a llif dy waed
Yn colli ei ffrwt, er gwaetha'r gorfoledd a gaed;

A phob greddf a chynneddf sy'n d'ysbryd er cyn co'
Yn mynd ar eu gwaeth – hwynt-hwythau'n disgwyl
eu tro.

Bydd dy iasau o ymgysegriad am ryw hyd
Efallai'n dal yn eu gwres, ond yn aros eu pryd.

Pan ddêl yr ymwrthod hwn megis trasiedi
A noethlymuno'r tu mewn i'th fodolaeth di,

Ni bydd dim yn aros ar ôl wedi'r ymwacáu
Ond tydi dy hun – a'r nos amdanat yn cau.

T.H. Parry-Williams

Poen

Dy boen yw torri'r plisgyn sy'n amgáu dy ddeall.
Megis y bydd yn rhaid i garreg ffrwyth chwalu er mwyn i'r cnewyllyn brofi gwres yr haul, felly mae'n rhaid i tithau adnabod poen.
Pe cedwit yn dy galon ryfeddod at wyrthiau beunyddiol dy fywyd, ni fyddai dy loes yn ymddangos ronyn yn llai o ryfeddod na'th lawenydd.
Derbyniet dymhorau dy galon fel y derbyniaist erioed dymhorau'r meysydd, a byddet yn barod i ddygymod yn raslon â gaeafau dy alar.

Kahlil Gibran

O lili wen fach

Hon oedd y gân ddiwethaf i ti ei dysgu,
ac fe welaist yr eirlysiau, y saffrwm a'r cennin pedr.

Er na pharhâi'n hir,
fe wrandewaist ar ddewrder yr un fach,
sy'n ernes yr haf.
Pan fyddet ti'n weddol,
doedd dim yn well gennyt na lliwio'n frwd,
holl liwiau'r prism, a darddodd, chwedl Waldo,
o'r gwynder glân.

Eithaf tristwch oedd dyddiau'r diwedd.
I ble'r ei di ar ddiwedd dy fywyd byr,
wrth ddechrau'r daith hwyaf o'r cwbl?
Y daith, yn ôl dy hoff Peter Pan,
a'th gofleidiodd ym myd Disney,
sy'n fenter arswydus fawr.

Yn dy lesgedd,
mae'r geiriau a fu'n gyfarwydd
yn dechrau rhydu ar dy wefus;
dy afael ar yr hen ganeuon yn gwanhau
a'r diwn yn llithro o'i lle,
a'r Gymraeg a goleddaist, ac a geraist yn dy alltudiaeth
  bell,
yn diflannu'n araf.
Ond y mae cof yn nyfnderoedd pob cân.

Anodd cyfaddef dy fod yn ddieithr bellach,
a bydd rhaid i ni dderbyn disgyblaeth enbyd yr ildio;
dy ildio i'r mawredd a'th roes.
Roedd gweld y geiriau, 'y dolur terfynol',
yn bwrw'r stumog, a brathu'r galon.

Rwyt ti, y wynnaf, yn wan iawn erbyn hyn,
a'th ocheneidiau ar obennydd yn amlhau.
Fe'th ildiwn, fe'th ildiwn,
i felystra tawelwch melodïau a chân.

Aled Gwyn

Llwch i'r Llwch

Diau rhan o'n daear ŷm,
Ychydig o lwch ydym,
I'r anfad a'r credadun
Mesur Duw yw amser dyn;
O bob gradd rhywbryd graddiwn
I'r unig radd a'r un grwn.

Cofier na roir y cyfan
Yn y blwch yn llwch y llan.
Bydd y cof yn boddi cur,
O hwn fe geisiwn gysur.
Try y llu adegau llon
Yn gyfoeth o atgofion;
Darn o hud o'r hyn a aeth
Ac sy'n aros yw'n hiraeth.

Idwal Lloyd

Gweddi'r Terfyn

Mae'n brofiad i bawb na ŵyr neb arall amdano.
Pob un ar ei ben ei hun yn ei ddull ei hun
Piau ei farw ei hun
Trwy filiynau blynyddoedd yr hil.
Gellir edrych arno, gellir weithiau adnabod yr eiliad;
Ni ellir cydymdeimlo â neb yn yr eiliad honno
Pan baid yr anadlu a'r person ynghyd.
Wedyn? Nid oes yn ymestyn i'r wedyn ond gweddi'n
  ymbalfalu.
Mor druan yw dyn, mor faban ei ddychymyg:
'Yn nhŷ fy Nhad y mae llawer o drigfannau',
Cyn dloted â ninnau, yr un mor ddaearol gyfyng
Oedd ei athrylith yntau ddyddiau yr ymwacâd.
Ninnau ni fedrwn ond felly ddarlunio gobaith:
'Mae'n eistedd ar ddeheulaw Dduw Dad hollalluog',–
Cadfridog a'i orfoledd drwy ddinas Rufain
Wedi'r enbydrwydd mewn Persia o greadigaeth
A'i goroni'n Awgwstws, Cyd-Awgwstws â'i Dad,–
Mor ddigri yw datganiadau goruchaf ein ffydd.
Ac o'n cwmpas erys mudandod a'r pwll diddymdra
Y syrth ein bydysawd iddo'n gyfan ryw nos.
Ni all ein geiriau olrhain ymylon mudandod
Na dweud Duw gydag ystyr.
Un weddi sy'n aros i bawb, mynd yn fud at y mud.

Saunders Lewis

Epigram

Lle bo galar yn aros,
para'n hir wna lampau'r nos.

Tudur Dylan Jones

Epigram

Mae alaw pan ddistawo
Yn mynnu canu'n y co'.

Dic Jones

Rhaid i ti fyned
y ffordd honno
dy hun

Hen linell bell, nad yw'n bod

Mae cariad yn dragwyddol; gorwel yn unig yw marwolaeth, ac nid yw gorwel yn ddim ond terfyn eithaf llygad dyn.

Rossiter W. Raymond

Y Llusern a'r Goleuni

Nid diffodd y goleuni y mae marwolaeth,
Ond diffodd llusern ar doriad gwawr.

Rabindranath Tagore

Peidiwch â diffygio

Peidiwch â diffygio; er chwerwed taith bywyd a'i diwedd anghyrraedd, nid oes un llwybr nad oes terfyn iddo.

Anhysbys

Marwnad o Dirdeunaw

(Detholiad)

Y mae angau'n gwahanu, ond eto'n ymgynnull ynghyd;
Y mae angau yn datod, ond eto'n ailgydio'r rhwygiadau;
Y mae angau'n ysgaru, ond eto'n ein closio i gyd
At ein gilydd, yn gwlwm mewn galar, yn unedig o fewn y rhaniadau.

Alan Llwyd

Angau

Rwyf wedi gweld angau yn rhy fynych i gredu mewn marwolaeth.
Nid diwedd yw, ond ymgilio:
Fel teithiwr yn cyrraedd pen ei daith,
Yn distewi'r modur, diffodd y goleuadau,
Camu o'r car,
A throedio'r llwybr i'w gartref tragwyddol.

Anhysbys

Gadael

Gadael modrwyau, cof bod yn briod,
Gadael poer a chwmni tafod.
Gadael enw, anghofio llofnod,
Gadael clyw, hen gysur myfyrdod.
Gadael anadlu, pob dawn adnabod.
Gadael y gollwng a gochel gwybod.
Gadael ymadael. Peidio peidio â bod.

Gwyneth Lewis

Mesur Dyn

Pan gaiff dyn ei fesur, gofynnir gan Dduw
Nid sut y gwnaeth farw, ond sut y gwnaeth fyw.

Nid faint a wnaeth ennill, ond faint fyddai'n rhoi,
Ac a fyddai yn aros pan oedd eraill yn ffoi.

Nid beth oedd ei gred ond beth fyddai'n ei wneud,
A faint oedd e'n teimlo, nid faint allai'i ddweud.

Nid uchder ei feddwl, ond dyfnder ei ras
A'i gymeriad tu fewn, nid ei wên y tu fas.

Nid faint oedd y deyrnged gan bawb i hen ffrind,
Ond faint deimlodd golled ar ôl iddo fynd.

Mae'n dda dweud na allai fyth golli'r un cwrdd,
Ond gwell dweud na throai 'run truan i ffwrdd,

Ac y bu yn oleuni mewn ambell i nos,
A throchi ei hun i ddwyn cyfaill o'r ffos.

Ie, dyna'n y diwedd y modd y gwêl Duw
Pa enaid sy'n farw a pha enaid sy'n fyw.

John Gwilym Jones

Addasiad o gerdd 'The Measure of Man' gan awdur anhysbys.

Dydy marw'n ddim

Dydy marw'n ddim . . .
dim ond wedi diflannu i'r ystafell nesaf ydw i . . .
rwy'n dal 'run fath fel yr wyt tithau.
Beth bynnag oedd rhyngom ni
mae'n dal i fodoli.
Galwa fi yn ôl yr hen enw cyfarwydd,
siarada â fi'n hamddenol
fel yr arferet wneud.
Paid â newid dy lais o gwbl
nac ymroi i dristwch na phruddglwyf.
Chwardda fel y byddem yn chwerthin
wrth fwynhau gyda'n gilydd y digrif bethau.
Mwynha dy hun, gwena, meddylia amdana i,
gweddïa drosof i.
Gad i'm henw fod o hyd
yn enw byw ar yr aelwyd.
Dywed ef yn hollol naturiol
heb ôl cysgod drosto.
Yr un fath yw bywyd ag y bu erioed,
mae'r rhod yn troi yn ddi-dor.
Pam ddylwn i fod allan o'th feddwl oherwydd
   fy mod o'r golwg?
Disgwyl amdanat ti yr ydw i,
am ryw egwyl, yn rhywle agos,
dim ond rownd y gornel . . .
mae pob peth yn iawn.

Henry Scott Holland, addasiad Aled Lewis Evans

Y Gân Dragywydd

Nid yw o bwys pa bryd y torrir tannau
A fu'n crynhoi melyster byd i'r gân;
Pan ddelo'n ddiwedd byd i ti a minnau
Ni chyll y nos ei sêr na'r haul ei dân.
Llifeiria bywyd dros ein bedd i'r perthi,
A chyfyd llanw'r gwanwyn megis cynt;
Anfarwol yw'r llinynnau tra bo cerddi
Aberoedd Cymru'n crwydro yn y gwynt.
Pan dorro'r farn yn ymyl a'm dychrynu
A'm bygwth gan yr adar dur uwchben,
Ni phaid anthemau'r cread â'm diddanu
Ym murmur moroedd ac yn nail y pren.
Ni pheidia'r gân er torri'r tannau'n sarn,
A'n claddu yn adfeilion llosg y farn.

T. E. Nicholas

* Carcharwyd T. E. Nicholas oherwydd ei heddychiaeth ar ddechrau'r Ail Ryfel Byd. Treuliodd amser mewn carchardai yn Abertawe a Llundain lle y clywodd awyrennau'r Almaen yn dod i ollwng eu bomiau ar y ddwy ddinas. Y rhain yw'r 'adar dur uwchben'.

Y Llong

A minnau'n sefyll ger y lan, wele long yn cyweirio'i hwyliau gwynion ar gychwyn ei thaith i'r cefnfor glas. Mae'n lluniaidd a chadarn, ac fe'i gwyliaf hyd oni ddiflannodd fel smotyn o gwmwl gwyn dros y gorwel. Yn f'ymyl, ochneidia rhywun, 'Fe aeth!' Ond i ble? O'm golwg i yr aeth, dyna i gyd. Mae'n dal yr un mor hardd, yr un mor gryf, yr un mor llawn o'r llwyth a ddug i ben ei thaith. I'm llygaid i yr aeth yn ddim.

Ac ar yr union eiliad honno pan glywn 'Fe aeth!' gwn am lygaid eraill yn ei chanfod, a lleisiau llon yn tystio, 'Fe ddaeth!'

Peth fel hyn yw marw.

Yn seiliedig ar ddarn gan Victor Hugo

I Eirian, Siôn a Guto

Am dy alar galaraf – oherwydd
Dy hiraeth hiraethaf,
Yn fy enaid griddfanaf
Drosot ti, a chyd-dristâf.

Dic Jones

Cofio Catrin

Os deui byth i oedi uwch fy medd
Ac ing a hiraeth yn cynhyrfu'r hedd,
Cofia fy nwyf . . .

Cofia nad fi sydd yno yn y gro,
Fy ysbryd i a'r holl atgofion sydd ar ffo
Nid yma'r wyf . . .

Chwilia amdanaf pan fo'r nos yn toddi'n wawr
Neu'r machlud derfyn dydd yn anfarwoli'r awr –
Yno bwyf . . .

Wrth wrando ar giglo'r forwennol a'i chri
Sy'n llonni Bae Cemlyn, a glywi di fi'n
Llawn nwyf?

Neu yn y pelydryn sy'n torri trwy'r cwmwl du
I ddawnsio am ennyd yn wefr uwch su
Y don . . .

Ac yno'n Lôn Cana uwch carped y clychau glas
Yng nghoch bendigedig y ffesant, sy'n ias
Fel erioed . . .

Yng nghynnwrf adenydd sy'n curo wrth godi'n rhydd
Uwch poethder a blinder a meithder y dydd
Drwy'r coed . . .

Paid byth â dod i ollwng dagrau uwch fy medd,
Ond gad i hwyl a chwerthin yr atgofion darfu'r hedd.

Cen Williams

Cerdd a gyfansoddwyd ar gyfer Gwasanaeth Dathlu Bywyd Dr Catrin Prys Jones, brodor o'r Fali, Ynys Môn, a fu farw'n annhymig ar 4 Hydref 2006. Roedd Catrin yn ddarlithydd ifanc ym Mhrifysgol Cymru, Aberystwyth.

Cafwyd y syniad gwreiddiol o gerdd Saesneg gan filwr anadnabyddus.

Llawenydd a Thristwch

Dy lawenydd yw dy dristwch mewn drych.
Mae'r ffynnon lle tardd dy chwerthin weithiau'n llenwi â'th ddagrau
A sut arall y gallai fod?
Po ddyfnaf y loes i'th enaid, po fwyaf y lle i lawenydd.
Onid y cwpan sy'n dal dy win yw'r union gwpan a daniwyd yn ffwrn y crochenydd?
Ac onid y crwth sy'n gostegu storm yr enaid yw'r union bren a naddwyd â chŷn?
Pan fyddi'n llawen, sylla i ddwfn dy galon ac fe weli mai yr un yw'r hyn a barodd iti loes ag sy'n cynnal dy lawenydd.
Pan fyddi'n drist, sylla eto i ddwfn dy galon, ac fe weli, mewn gwirionedd, mai wylo yr wyt am yr hyn a fu gynt yn hyfrydwch i ti.

Kahlil Gibran

Hen yw'r sawl a ŵyr

Cysur Henaint

Mae mewn ieuenctid dristwch, ac mewn oed
Ddiddanwch, fel ar haul yr haf y trig
Y bore-ddydd yn dywyll yn y coed,
A'r nawnddydd fel y nos o dan y brig;
Nes dyfod mis o'r misoedd pan fo'r gwynt
Yn cychwyn crinddail ar eu hediad oer,
A thrwy'r dinefoedd dywyll-leoedd gynt
Yn chwythu llewych haul a llewych lloer.
Ninnau, pan syrth ein grawnwin, a phan dynn
Dydd ein diddychwel haf hyd eitha 'i rawd,
Ni wyddom beth a fyddwn, onid hyn:
Mor druan nid yw Henaint nac mor dlawd
Nad erys yn ei gostrel beth o'r gwin
I hybu'r galon rhwng yr esgyrn crin.

R. Williams Parry

Gormod

Ni fynnwn i gan fywyd mwy
Anwylo'n hir ei bethau chwim;
Un ennyd fer i'w profi hwy
Fydd bellach yn hen ddigon im.

Eiliad o aros yn y wledd,
Un ias o'i rhwysg, un rhan o'i rhin;
Rhag troi yn adflas hoen yr hedd,
Rhag pydru o'r ffrwyth a chwerwi o'r gwin.

Ni fynnwn faith anwesu serch
Er glynu ohono, dyn a ŵyr,
Rhag mynd o'i gur yn dwymyn erch
A'i ffynnon bêr yn syrffed llwyr

J. M. Edwards

Yr Hen a Ŵyr

Rwy'n ddigon hen i wybod erbyn hyn
Na phery prudd-der na dedwyddwch chwaith.
Cymysg yw'n bywyd ni, a'r du a'r gwyn
Yn dilyn yn eu tro ar hyd y daith.
Ni phery bri y dewr na'r cryf na'r chwim,
Ac eilun mwya'r dorf yn angof â;
Sêl pob gwrthryfel chwerw nid erys ddim, –
Daw barrug hydre' i bylu gwres yr ha'.

Nid oes hirhoedledd i orchestion dyn
Nac i gywreinrwydd celf na chrefft na chân.
Ni phery serch godidog llanc a bun,
Bydd mynych borthi'r fflam yn difa'r tân.
Hiraeth ni phery byth; er oedi'n hir;
Ond hen yw'r sawl a ŵyr fod hynny'n wir.

T. Llew Jones

Gobaith

Gobaith

Beth yw Gobaith? Y gwybod –
O dan y bai – fod da'n bod.

T. Llew Jones

Bydd yn wrol

Bydd yn wrol, paid â llithro,
er mor dywyll yw y daith
y mae seren i'th oleuo:
cred yn Nuw a gwna dy waith.
Er i'r llwybyr dy ddiffygio,
er i'r anial fod yn faith,
bydd yn wrol, blin neu beidio:
cred yn Nuw a gwna dy waith.

Paid ag ofni'r anawsterau,
paid ag ofni'r brwydrau chwaith;
paid ag ofni'r canlyniadau:
cred yn Nuw a gwna dy waith.
Cei dy farnu, cei dy garu,
cei dy wawdio lawer gwaith;
na ofala ddim am hynny:
cred yn Nuw a gwna dy waith.

Norman Macleod
cyf. Ben Davies

Tystiolaeth olaf Yosi Rakover

(*Yn adfeilion y Ghetto yn Warsaw, yn 1943, darganfuwyd, mewn potel a guddiwyd ymhlith cerrig llosg ac esgyrn dynol, y datganiad hwn a ysgrifennwyd yn ei oriau olaf gan yr Iddew Yosi Rakover.*)

Mae'r haul yn machlud a, diolch i Dduw, nis gwelaf byth eto. Mae goleuni'r tanau yn treiddio drwy'r ffenestr ac y mae'r darn bach o awyr a welaf yn goch tân fel rhaeadr waedlyd. Ymhen rhyw awr arall ar y mwyaf, byddaf yn ymuno â'm teulu a meirwon fy mhobl mewn byd gwell, heb amheuon mwyach, lle mae Duw yn teyrnasu.

Rwy'n marw mewn hedd, ond heb fy ngwastrodi, wedi fy ngorchfygu a'm curo ond heb fy narostwng, yn chwerw ond heb fy siomi, yn credu ond heb ymbilio, yn caru Duw ond heb chwaith ymgreinio'n ddall.

Dilynais Ef hyd yn oed pan y'm gwrthodwyd ganddo. Ufuddheais i'w orchmynion hyd yn oed pan gefais fy fflangellu am wneud hynny. Fe'i cerais a bûm mewn cariad ag Ef a pharhaf felly hyd yn oed pan y'm darostyngir yn is na llwch y llawr, pan y'm poenydir hyd at angau, a'm gadael i ddioddef pob gwarth a dirmyg.

Dyma fy ngeiriau olaf wrthyt Ti fy Nuw dicllon: Ni thycia ddim o hyn oll. Gwnaethost bopeth i chwalu fy ffydd ynot Ti, ac i ddifa fy nghred. Ond rwy'n marw yn union fel y bûm byw, yn grediniwr digymrodedd ynot Ti.

Moled yn awr Dduw'r meirwon, Duw dial, Duw gwirionedd a barn, a ddatguddia eto, cyn hir, ei wyneb i'r byd a siga'r sylfeini â'i lef nerthol.

I'th ddwylo di o Dduw y cyflwynaf fy enaid.

Mae gennyf freuddwyd

Mae gennyf freuddwyd, ryw ddydd y bydd y genedl hon yn codi ac yn byw gwirionedd ei chred
'Credwn fod gwirioneddau fel hyn yn rhai amlwg, fod pob dyn wedi'i greu yn gyfartal.'
Mae gennyf freuddwyd, ryw ddydd y bydd meibion caethweision a meibion eu meistri yn eistedd ynghyd wrth fwrdd brawdgarwch, ar fryniau coch Georgia.
Mae gennyf freuddwyd y bydd hyd yn oed Talaith Mississippi, talaith anial sy'n chwysu ym mhoethder anghyfiawnder a gormes, yn cael ei gweddnewid yn werddon o ryddid a chyfiawnder.
Mae gennyf freuddwyd y bydd fy mhedwar plentyn, ryw ddydd, yn rhan o genedl lle bernir hwy, nid yn ôl lliw eu croen ond yn ôl natur eu cymeriad.
Mae gennyf freuddwyd, heddiw.

Martin Luther King

Mae gennyf freuddwyd, heddiw

(Detholiad)

(Martin Luther King)

Mae gen i freuddwyd am y wlad
Lle bydd pawb yn bobol,
Lle na fydd gormes na nacâd
Na chas byth mwy dragwyddol.

Mae gen i freuddwyd am y wlad
Lle bydd diwedd angau,
Lle na fydd cynnen, trais, na brad,
Lle na fydd ofn cadwynau.

Mae gen i freuddwyd am y wlad
Lle bydd cariad yno,
Lle na fydd dicter mwy, na llid,
Lle na fydd neb yn wylo.

A disglair ydyw'r muriau mawr
A hardd fel môr o wydyr
A'r pyrth a egyr yn y wawr
I fyd a fu ar grwydyr.

Mae ar hyd yn oed ddynion lludw,
Du eu lliw, eisiau byw.

Gwyn Thomas

Yfory

Gwthiaf fy nghwch i'r dŵr yfory
O gilfach gyntefig deisyfiad dyn,
Ymhell o 'stumiau'r dref a'i stŵr;
Ac ni bydd un dyddiol dasg i'm carcharu
Na'i bryder na bref ei loi aur i'm halaru,
Na thŷ na theulu a'u dôr i'm daearu,
Na neb i'm hysgwyd o freuddwyd a hun
Yfory, pan wthiaf fy nghwch i'r dŵr.

Codaf fy hwyl i'r gwynt yfory
O borthladd bach nas darganfu'r byd,
Ynghlo yn fy nghwch mae dirgelwch fy hynt;
Byr fydd y boen os gyr ein hysgaru
Air o gerydd o'r lle bu hir garu,
Neu weiddi eirias i geisio 'myddaru
Rhag islais melys a'm tywys i'm tud
Yfory, pan godaf fy hwyl i'r gwynt.

Moriaf ymhell o dir yfory
Heb undyn a ŵyr lle bydd terfyn taith
Na dolef a'm dilyn, boed fer, boed hir;
Os awel a eiria'r atgofus alaru
Ar y du fôr, ni bydd edifaru,
Awelon eraill a ddaw i liniaru
Ellyllon cyndyn y cof wrth eu gwaith
Yfory, pan foriaf ymhell o dir.

Caradog Prichard

Cymod a chyflawn we . . .

Datganiad yr Archesgob Desmond Tutu gerbron Pwyllgor Cymod a Gwirionedd De Affrica

Byddwn wedi syllu i fyw llygaid yr anghenfil. Byddwn wedi dygymod â'n gorffennol brawychus ac ni fyddwn yn wystl iddo mwyach. Datodwn ei hualau a chan gydio law yn llaw, yn groenddu a chroenwyn, brasgamwn – nyni bobl yr Enfys – i'r dyfodol, y dyfodol gogoneddus a addewir gan Dduw, a chan edrych yn ôl ar ein gorffennol, ymdynghedwn: Byth eto!

Archesgob Desmond Tutu

Gweddi

Arglwydd daioni'r flwyddyn – cymoda'r
  Cymydog â'i elyn.
 Di geidwad anghredadun
 Atal Di wanc teulu dyn.

Yn nyddiau'r drin bydd Di'n dŵr – i'th bobol
  A'th babell yn swcwr.
 Bydd loches rhag gormeswr,
 Dyro nawdd i druan ŵr.

Rho o hyd i blant pryder – dy nodded
  Yn nydd eu cyfyngder,
 Ac yn ei ofn, plyg, ein Nêr
 Y byd i ddweud ei bader.

Dig y byd o dwg i ben – dilea
  O'i deuluoedd angen.
 Dros ein gwlad rho dy aden
 Er mwyn dy Enw mawr, Amen.

Dic Jones

Tangnefedd

Distawrwydd a Thawelwch

Ni cheir tawelwch oni byddo'r ysbryd mewn cynghanedd gyfriniol â'r distawrwydd o'i gwmpas. Rhaid yw bod distawrwydd oddi mewn yn ateb i'r distawrwydd oddi allan, ac y mae cysegredigrwydd lle yn gymorth gwerthfawr i gynhyrchu yn ysbryd dyn yr hyn a dry'r distawrwydd oddi allan yn dawelwch oddi mewn . . . Amgylchiadau sy'n peri distawrwydd, ond ysbryd dyn yn unig a fedr dynnu o'r distawrwydd dawelwch. Peth i'r glust yw distawrwydd; peth i'r galon yw tawelwch. O gwmpas dyn y mae'r naill; o'i fewn y mae'r llall . . .

John Owen (Morfa Nefyn)

Emyn

Rho im yr hedd na ŵyr y byd amdano,
hedd, nefol hedd, a ddaeth drwy ddwyfol loes;
pan fyddo'r don ar f'enaid gwan yn curo
mae'n dawel gyda'r Iesu wrth y groes.

O rho yr hedd na all y stormydd garwaf
ei flino byth na chwerwi ei fwynhad
pan fyddo'r enaid ar y noson dduaf
yn gwneud ei nyth ym mynwes Duw ein Tad.

Rho brofi'r hedd a wna im weithio'n dawel
yng ngwaith y nef dan siomedigaeth flin;
heb ofni dim, ond aros byth yn ddiogel
yng nghariad Duw, er garwed fyddo'r hin.

O am yr hedd sy'n llifo megis afon
drwy ddinas Duw, dan gangau'r bywiol bren:
hedd wedi'r loes i dyrfa'r pererinion
heb gwmwl byth na nos, tu hwnt i'r llen.

Elfed

Myfyrdod

Rhowch i mi gilfach a glan,
Cilfach a glan a marian i mi,
Lle na ddaw'r gwylanod ar gyfyl y fan,
Na mwstwr tonnau nwydus, twyllodrus y lli.

Ymhell o'r storm a'i stŵr,
Y storm a'i stŵr a'i dwndwr a'i gwawd,
Lle na ddaw'r gwyntoedd i boeni'r dŵr,
Na'r cesair creulon i daro, cnocio'r cnawd.

Lle na ddaw'r geifr â'u cyrn,
Y geifr â'u cyrn hëyrn a hir,
Na phystylad meirch porthiannus, chwyrn,
A'u carnau carlam i godi, torri'r tir.

Rhyw ddedwydd lonydd le,
Llonydd le ar dyle neu dwyn,
Lle caf fodio llawysgrifau'r ne,
Dethol gyfrolau'r doethion, mynachdod myfyrdod
mwyn.

D. Gwenallt Jones

Fy Nymuniad

Pan wyt yn unig
dymunaf Gariad i ti;

pan wyt yn drist
dymunaf Hapusrwydd i ti;

pan fydd pethau'n dy boeni
dymunaf Dangnefedd i ti;

pan mae pethau'n gymhleth
dymunaf i ti weld Harddwch syml;

pan fydd pethau'n ymddangos yn dywyll,
dymunaf i ti Obaith.

addas. Aled Lewis Evans

Gweddi Milwr

Gofynnais am nerth fel y gallwn lwyddo;
Fe'm gwnaed yn wan fel y dysgwn ufuddhau yn ostyngedig.
Gofynnais am iechyd fel y gallwn gyflawni pethau mawr;
Rhoddwyd imi lesgedd fel y gallwn gyflawni pethau gwell.
Gofynnais am olud fel y gallwn fod yn hapus;
Rhoddwyd imi dlodi fel y gallwn fod yn ddoeth.
Gofynnais am bopeth fel y gallwn fwynhau bywyd;
Rhoddwyd imi fywyd fel y gallwn fwynhau popeth.
Ni dderbyniais ddim y gofynnais amdano:
Ond derbyniais y cyfan y gobeithiwn amdano.

Gweddi milwr dienw
addas. Owain Llyr Evans

Hapus Dyrfa

Gwêl uwchlaw cymylau amser,
O fy enaid, gwêl y tir
Lle mae'r awel fyth yn dyner,
Lle mae'r wybren fyth yn glir.
Hapus dyrfa
Sydd yn nofio yn ei hedd.

Nid oes yno neb yn wylo
Yno nid oes neb yn brudd,
Troir yn fêl y wermod yno,
Yno rhoir y caeth yn rhydd;
Hapus dyrfa
Sydd â'u trigfa yno mwy.

Islwyn

Bendith Geltaidd

'Boed Tangnefedd y dyfnder mawr i chi
Boed Tangnefedd y sêr uwchben,
Boed Tangnefedd yr awel fwyn i chi
Boed Tangnefedd y ddaear hen.
Boed hedd yn dy enaid di
Gad i hedd lanw dy fywyd di.'

addas. Aled Lewis Evans

Gweddi Sant Ffransis o Assisi

'Bydded cariad lle bu casineb,
Bydded gobaith lle bu anobaith
A lle bu amheuaeth bydded ffydd.
Bydded cysur lle bu galar
A llawenydd lle bu tristwch,
A lle bu tywyllwch megis nos
Boed goleuni megis ffydd.'

addas. Tecwyn Ifan

Cyngor Porthor y Flwyddyn

Cyferchais y gŵr a safai ar riniog y flwyddyn: 'Rho imi lusern i rodio'n ddiogel i'r yfory.' Meddai ef, 'Dos allan i'r tywyllwch a chydia yn llaw dy Dduw. Bydd hyn yn rhagorach i ti na'r un llusern ac yn fwy diogel na'r un ffordd gyfarwydd.'

Minnie Louise Haskins

Y Canol Llonydd Distaw

Dal fi'n dynn . . . paid dweud dim . . .

Gwawriodd arnaf i o'r diwedd un o wersi Tao Te Ching
mai gwacter, llonydd a heddwch a distawrwydd sydd wrth wraidd pob dim
ond glywi di y cegau yn siarad?
glywi di y lleisiau mor groch?
maen nhw'n debyg i minnau yn malu awyr
yn debyg i chdithau yn f'ateb innau
'dan ni'n swnio fel miloedd o wenyn prysur
weithia' fel storom o fellt a tharanau.

Dal fi'n dynn . . . paid dweud dim . . .
Dwi'n chwilio am y canol llonydd distaw
sy ynof fi fy hun ac ynghanol pob dim,
chwilio am y gwacter mawr a hyfryd
ynom ni i gyd yn llonydd fel llyn

'Dan ni'n hau hadau, medi'r cnydau Daw tymor arall i aredig
Gobeithio bod ni'n dysgu rywsut Sut i fyw yn fwy caredig . . .
weli di dy ffrindiau'n chwilio
yng nghanol y wyneba' di-ri'
am un edrychiad, un cyffyrddiad
rhyw sylweddoliad, darganfyddiad,
'dan ni angen edrych i fyw llygaid ein gilydd
angen dinoethi heb deimlo c'wilydd

Gwyn eu byd y rhai sy'n noeth . . .
Yn chwilio am y canol llonydd distaw
sy ynof fi fy hun ac ynghanol pob dim,
chwilio am y gwacter mawr a hyfryd
ynom ni i gyd yn llonydd fel llyn

Noson gynnes yng Ngorffennaf, yr haul yn machlud
   dros y ffin
ffrindiau wrth y bwrdd yn chwerthin rhannu sgwrs a
   chaws a gwin
mae y trefi mawr a'r dinasoedd
yn pwyso'n rhy drwm arnom ni
'dan ni angen llwybr mewn coedwig dawel
mwsog a nentydd, mymryn o awel
angen gollwng baich y geiriau
a chlywed ochenaid y Fam Ddaear

Gwyn eu byd yr addfwyn rai . . .
Sy'n chwilio am y canol llonydd distaw
sy ynof fi fy hun ac ynghanol pob dim,
chwilio am y gwacter mawr a hyfryd
ynom ni i gyd yn llonydd fel llyn

Steve Eaves

Ystafell Fewnol

Mae gen i ddyfnder
na fydda i'n ei ddangos
i'm ffrindiau'n aml iawn,
rhyw ddistawrwydd
sydd y tu hwnt i'r miri,
yn ddyfnach
na thrio bod yn ddiddorol.

Mae'n ystafell o ryfeddodau
yn y fi go iawn,
sy'n llawer mwy cyffyrddus,
fel hen slipars.
Ond mae'n brifo
gadael pobl mewn i fanno
rhag ofn iddyn nhw
adael y stafell
mewn chwip o dymer
un dydd.
Gadael llanast a'r drws ar agor i'r oerwynt
sy'n sobri.

Ond mae'r ystafell yno
y tu ôl i'r llygaid,
ac mae'n lle braf
nid fel y tu allan
lle mae'n rhaid bodloni
bod yn galed,
dilyn rôl
fel mae'r mêts yn disgwyl.

Ond ar ddiwedd y dydd
pan does neb o gwmpas,
caf gilio yno'n dawel
ac wynebu neb ond fi fy hun.

Y fi sy tu ôl i'r llygaid
y fi rwyt ti
(efallai)
yn gallu'i weld.

Aled Lewis Evans

Beati Mortui

Mor ddedwydd yw y rhai trwy ffydd
Sy'n mynd o blith y byw;
Eu henwau'n perarogli sydd,
A'u hun, mor dawel yw.

Ar ôl eu holl flinderau dwys
Gorffwyso maent mewn hedd,
Ymhell o sŵn y byd a'i bwys,
Heb boen yn llwch y bedd.

Llais un gorthrymydd byth ni ddaw
I'w deffro i wylo mwy,
Na phrofedigaeth lem, na chroes,
Un loes ni theimlant hwy.

Ieuan Glan Geirionydd

Cymdeithas dyn a dyn

I'm Cydnabod

Mae rhywbeth yng nghymdeithas dyn a dyn
Sy'n aros wedi'r ymwahano'r ddau.
Pan gyfyd law ffarwelio nid yr un
Yw'r naill na'r llall ohonynt. Cans bu hau
O'r ddeutu ffrwyth profiadau'r hir grynhoi,
I fyw neu farw, yn efrau ac yn ŷd,
Bu ffeirio gwên am heulwen, a bu rhoi
A derbyn anobeithion yr un pryd.
Nid aeth na gwên na gwg na dawn a roed
I ddyn ar goll er pan fu'r cyntaf gwawr,
Pob crefft a aeth o ddyn i ddyn erioed,
Yn rhywun, rhywle, maent i gyd ar glawr.
Fy niolch i'm cydnabod o bob gwaed,
Hwynt-hwy yw'r deunydd crai o'r hwn y'm gwnaed.

Dic Jones

Geiriau Tecumseh, un o benaethiaid llwyth y Shawnee yn 1795

Carreg yw'm calon
yn drom gan dristwch fy mhobl,
oer
yn y sicrwydd na saif cyfamod
a geidw'r gwyn eu crwyn o'n tiroedd,
caled
o benderfyniad i wrthsefyll
tra bo anadl ynof.
Yr ydym heddiw yn wan a'n pobl yn ofnus
ond gwrandewch ar fy ngeiriau.

'Torri wna'r brigyn unig;
Cryfder yw plethiad canghennau;
Daw dydd y cofleidiaf lwythi fy hil
a'u plethu'n frenhinbren.
Enillwn yr erwau'n ôl,
y rhai a feddiannwyd
gan y gwyn eu crwyn.'

Arfon Huws

Cyfaill

Mae fy ngobeithion yn rhan ohonot,
Mae fy nioddef a'm hofnau'n eiddot,
Yn d'oriau euraid, fy malchder erot,
Yn d'oriau isel, fy ngweddi drosot,
Mae'n well byd y man lle bôt, – mae deunydd
Fy holl lawenydd, fy nghyfaill, ynot.

Dic Jones

Plentyn y Ddaear

(Detholiad)

Daw dydd y bydd mawr y rhai bychain,
Daw dydd ni bydd mwy y rhai mawr,
Daw'r bore ni wêl ond brawdoliaeth
Yn casglu teuluoedd y llawr.
O ogofâu'r nos y cerddasom
I'r gwynt am a gerddai ein gwaed;
Tosturi, O sêr, uwch ein pennau,
Amynedd, O bridd, dan ein traed.

Waldo Williams

Geiriau Pastor Niemoeller

I ddechrau daethant am yr Iddewon
ac ni chodais fy llais –
achos doeddwn i ddim yn Iddew.

Yna daethant am y comiwnyddion
ac ni chodais fy llais –
achos doeddwn i ddim yn gomiwnydd.

Yna daethant am yr undebwyr llafur
ac ni chodais fy llais
gan nad oeddwn yn undebwr llafur.

Yna daethant amdana i –
ond doedd neb ar ôl
i godi llais ar fy rhan i.

addas. Aled Lewis Evans

Addewid ar Ddiwrnod Cofio'r Holocost

Mae'r frwydr dros degwch yn dechrau gyda fi,
A dyw'r gwir ddim yn bod os na fedraf i ei ddweud.
Dydw i ddim yn iach tra bo eraill yn gaeth.
Mae cyfiawnder yn ddrud, ond gwnaf ei waith.

Rwy'n gwrthod ofni
Casineb a thrais.
Chwynnaf eu celwyddau fel drain
A phlannu haelioni yn flodau cain.

Os trof fy nghefn, pwy a fyn hawliau
i eraill, fel y rhai rwy'n eu mwynhau?
Dydw i ddim yn iach tra bo eraill yn gaeth.
Mae cyfiawnder yn ddrud ond gwnaf ei waith.

Gwyneth Lewis

Yr Elfen Odidocaf a Pheryclaf

Geiriau Toyohiko Kagawa

'Nid oes gennyf ond un efengyl, sef yw honno,
yr ailenir popeth drwy gariad.
Cariad yn unig sy'n hollalluog.
Cariad yn unig sy'n dragwyddol.
Cariad a greodd y byd.
Cariad sy'n ei gynnal.
Cariad yw hanfod Duw . . .
Y mae Cariad yn egluro popeth.
Cariad yw fy nghysegr sancteiddiolaf i.
Trwy gariad yr wyf yn esgyn i'r uchelderau,
ac yn disgyn i'r dyfnderoedd.
Y mae Cariad yn treiddio trwy bopeth . . .
 llygad rhyfeddol cariad
mae Duw a dyn yn canfod ei gilydd.
Mewn cariad fe dry llygad dyn yn llygad Duw.
Mewn Cariad y daw duwdod a dyndod yn un.'

addas. T. Glyn Thomas

Gwir Natur Nerth

Bu'r Iesu farw fel y gwnaeth i'n dysgu – i ddysgu'r ddynoliaeth i iawn-ddeall yr elfen odidocaf a pheryclaf ei phosibiliadau a roddwyd yn ei dwylo, sef nerth. Bu farw'n ddiymadferth i'n herio allan o'n ffordd fabanaidd o ddeall nerth, sef yn nhermau diogelwch, yn nhermau troi nerth yn gaer o'n hamgylch i gadw'r gelyn draw.

I'r ofnus, babanaidd, 'deuddeng lleng o angylion' ydyw nerth. Ond fel arall y syniai ef – 'Nac wylwch o'm plegid i.' Yr oedd o'n gwybod beth oedd o'n ei wneud. Cario allan i'r pen ydoedd y gwaith o ddangos i ddynion cibddall sut un ydyw Duw, sut beth yw ei fawredd a'i allu mewn gwirionedd; dal i ddangos i'r pen bod yr unig Un y mae ganddo awdurdod diamodol dros fodolaeth y byd, yn dewis bod yn ddiallu yn y byd – yn gwbl ddiymadferth yn nwylo dynion – er mwyn dysgu dynion y wers bwysicaf a oedd ganddynt i'w dysgu yn wyneb posibiliadau eu deall a'u dyfeisgarwch . . .

O gynysgaeddu creadur meidrol â'r deall a'r dyfeisgarwch a berthyn i ddyn, yr oedd yn bod o'r cychwyn, gan hynny, bosibilrwydd y câi hwn rywbryd afael ar bwerau a'i blotiai allan o fod oni ddysgai'r wers bwysig mewn pryd, sef beth yw gwir natur nerth, beth yw gwir allu gallu – mai'r gallu i ffrwyno gallu ym mhlaid creu ydyw, mai'r gallu i greu ydyw'r gallu mawr ac mai cariad, gan hynny, yw'r gwir allu.

J. R. Jones

Tystiolaeth Corrie Ten Boom

(*Yn 1947 bu'n rhaid i Corrie Ten Boom wynebu un a fu'n ei phoenydio a'i harteithio yn y gwersylloedd crynhoi. Gofynnodd iddi am faddeuant.*)

Roedd yn rhaid i mi ei wneud o, roeddwn i'n gwybod hynny. Mae'r neges fod Duw yn maddau efo amod i ni: ein bod ni'n maddau i'r bobl sydd wedi'n brifo ni. Yn ôl Iesu, 'Os na wnewch chi faddau i bobl eu dyledion, ni fydd eich Tad yn y nefoedd yn maddau i chi.'

Roeddwn i'n dal i sefyll yno efo'r oerfel yn gafael am fy nghalon. Ond mae maddeuant yn codi o awydd, a gall yr awydd ddal i fod er gwaethaf tymheredd y galon. 'Iesu, helpa fi' gweddïais yn dawel. 'Fedra i godi fy llaw. Fedra i wneud cymaint â hynny. Rho Di y teimlad i mi.'

Felly yn brennaidd a mecanyddol taflais fy llaw at yr un oedd yn disgwyl amdana i. Ac wrth i mi wneud, fe ddigwyddodd rhywbeth rhyfeddol iawn. Cychwynnodd cerrynt o gynhesrwydd yn fy ysgwydd, saethodd i lawr fy mraich, a chyrraedd lle'r oedd ein dwy law yn uno. A daeth y cynhesrwydd gwellhad yma i lenwi fy holl fodolaeth, gan dynnu dagrau i'm llygaid.

'Dwi'n maddau i ti, fy mrawd,' gwaeddais innau, 'gyda'm holl galon.'

Am ennyd hir gafaelom am ddwylo ein gilydd – y cyn-gard a'r cyn-garcharor. Doeddwn i erioed wedi adnabod cariad Duw mor deimladol ag yr oeddwn wedi gwneud y pryd hynny.

addas. Aled Lewis Evans

Rhywun yn siglo'r cread

Yr Alaw

Anaml y'i clywir cyn y terfyn
ond fe'i teimlais y bore o'r blaen yn yr ardd
pan drodd y llwydrew'r berllan yn wyn,

y coed fel deltas du a chân
y fwyalchen mor ddiffrwyth â cherrig.
Roedd y golch wedi rhewi'n dafodau tân

yn cusanu'r oerfel ac, fel y symudwn,
gafaelem mewn gwreichion, ein hanadl gwyn
yn gymylau prysur fel swigod cartŵn

ond yn wag o eiriau. Gweithiwn yn ddistaw,
fel pe bai'r caddug wedi diffodd y byd
a phopeth am ennyd, ond am yr alaw

sy'n rhuddin ein bywyd, cyweirnod llwm –
heb liw, heb wres, heb rodres haul –
y dôn sy'n ffynnon ynom,

nid hawdd ei llygru, mesur glân
pob peth sy'n werthfawr. Er gorchuddio'r byd
â mwrllwch, mae gorfoledd hon

yn ŵyl i'w dathlu, yn gyhydnos ha'
yng nghanol gaea'. Tyrd yma 'nghariad,
paid â gofyn pam, tyrd yma . . .

Gwyneth Lewis

Weithiau

Rwy' weithiau, er pob dadrithiad, rywfodd
yn profi cyffyrddiad
rhywun yn siglo'r cread
yn fwyn iawn, fel llaw fy nhad.

Emyr Lewis

'This great absence that is like a presence'

Ildio i'r absenoldeb a wna pawb,
fel pos heb ei ateb
yn iawn; ys gwn i wnaeth Neb
ildio i'w bresenoldeb?

Emyr Lewis

Grym Ysbrydol

Nid dyma'r tro olaf i mi sylwi yn yr India y modd y mae profiad mewnol crefyddol yn ei fynegi ei hun mewn disgleirdeb wyneb ac mewn dylanwadau sy'n hawdd i'w teimlo er yn anweledig. Sylwais arno nid yn unig mewn enghreifftiau Cristnogol ond hefyd mewn canlynwyr crefyddau eraill. Ym mhob achos y mae'r dyn ohono'i hun wedi ymryddhau a grym ysbrydol y cread ar orsedd ei fywyd mewnol, pa enw bynnag a rydd i hwnnw. Ac ymhob achos hyd y gallwn farnu rhedodd y grym ysbrydol hwnnw fel afon y bywyd trwyddynt yn ffrydiau iachusol i ddyfrhau a chyfoethogi bywydau trueiniaid o'u cwmpas. Ond fe welais law farwol ofergoeliaeth hefyd a phla angheuol paganiaeth er nad yw'r rheiny yn absennol yng Nghymru na nepell oddi wrth bawb ohonom. Y prawf i mi o aeddfedrwydd ysbrydol, ym mha ddiwylliant bynnag y bo a pha idiom bynnag a ddefnyddir i'w fynegi, yw calon dosturiol yn cynhyrchu maddeugarwch graslon a gweithredoedd hunanaberthol a chariadlon.

Cyril G. Williams

Pob peth yn Bod

Mae pob peth yn bod,
ac ni all un ochenaid
na gwên na deigryn,
na blewyn na dernyn o lwch –
ni all yr un ohonynt –
ddarfod.

Willam Blake

Ystyriwch heddiw'r dydd

Ystyriwch heddiw'r dydd! Oherwydd hwn yw bywyd, bywyn pob bywyd. Breuddwyd yw ddoe a rhith yw yfory. Ond y mae heddiw, o'i fyw yn iawn, yn gwneud pob ddoe yn freuddwyd o hapusrwydd ac yfory yn addewid o obaith. Ystyriwch yn ddwys felly heddiw'r dydd.

Dihareb Sanscrit

Gweled Nef ym Mhlygion Blodyn

Gweled nef ym mhlygion blodyn,
Canfod byd mewn un tywodyn,
Dal mewn orig dragwyddoldeb,
Cau dy ddwrn am anfeidroldeb.

T. Gwynn Jones
efelychiad o William Blake

Nid oes yng ngwreiddyn Bod un wywedigaeth
Yno mae'n rhuddin yn parhau.
Yno mae'r dewrder sy'n dynerwch
Bywyd pob bywyd brau.

Yno wedi'r ystorom y cilia'r galon.
Mae'r byd yn chwâl,
Ond yn yr isel gaer mae gwiwer gwynfyd
Heno yn gwneud ei gwâl.

Waldo Williams

Diolchiadau

Diolchaf i'r cyfeillion canlynol am eu sylwadau a'u cyfraniadau wrth i mi lunio'r gyfrol:

Roger Jones Williams, cyn-Gyfarwyddwr Addysg Ceredigion, a Desmond Healy a ddarllenodd y gyfrol a'm hannog i ddal ati. Diolch i'm cyfaill Dewi Hughes am gyflwyno i mi waith Kahlil Gibran. Diolch i Bethan Mair, a welodd bosibiliadau'r gyfrol hon, ac i Rhiannon Davies, golygyddion cydnaws Gwasg Gomer. Mae gennyf ddiolch arbennig i'm gwraig Delyth am ei holl waith mireinio ar y deunydd a gyfieithais. Roeddwn yn ymdopi â pheintio'r wal, fel petai, ond hi oedd yn gofalu am gywreinrwydd yr addurniadau.

Mynegai

Oni nodir yn wahanol, eiddo D. Geraint Lewis yw'r addasiadau i'r Gymraeg o weithiau a gyhoeddwyd yn wreiddiol mewn ieithoedd eraill.

Cydnabyddiaethau

Bu'n her cael at wraidd ffynhonnell pob dyfyniad; ceisiwyd, lle roedd hynny'n ymarferol, gael caniatâd pob deiliad hawlfraint ond ni lwyddwyd ym mhob achos. Nid bwriad Gwasg Gomer oedd tramgwyddo, a byddem yn falch o dderbyn gwybodaeth am berchnogion hawliau nas cydnabuwyd er mwyn gallu cywiro'r ailargraffiad.

Dymunir cydnabod y ffynonellau isod:

Cyhoeddiadau Barddas: *Apocalups Yfory* 'Dyfod', Gwyn Thomas; *Chwarae Mig* 'Yr Efengyl yn Ôl Rusty James', 'Llwy Garu', Emyr Lewis; *Tair Mewn Un* 'Hanner', 'Gadael', 'Yr Alaw', Gwyneth Lewis; *Cerddi Alan Llwyd* 'I'm Mab', 'Marwnad o Dirdeunaw', Alan Llwyd; *Adenydd* 'Cysur', 'Epigram', Tudur Dylan Jones; *Cyn i'r Dydd Hwyrhau* 'Amser', D. Islwyn Edwards; *Sglefrfyrddio* 'Ystafell Fewnol', Aled Lewis Evans.

Cyhoeddiadau'r Gair: *Troeon* 'Dydy Marw'n Ddim', 'Fy Nymuniad', 'Bendith Geltaidd', 'Geiriau Pastor Niemoeller', 'Tystiolaeth Corrie Ten Boom', Aled Lewis Evans; 'Geiriau Toyohiko Kagawa', T. Glyn Thomas; 'Gweddi Sant Ffransis o Assisi', Tecwyn Ifan; *O'r Tŷ i'r tŷ* 'Gweddi Milwr', Owain Llyr Evans.

Gwasg Carreg Gwalch: *Pen Draw'r Tir* 'Graffiti yn Pompeii', 'Cariad', Myrddin ap Dafydd; *Llain yn Llŷn* 'Geiriau Crowfoot ar ei wely angau', 'Geiriau

Tecumseh, un o benaethiaid y Shawnee', Arfon Huws; *Y Grefft o Dan-y-Groes* 'Cyfaill', Ken Griffiths; *Amser Amherffaith/ Dysgu Dweud Celwydd yn Tsiec* 'Weithiau', '*This Great Absence that is like a Presence*', Emyr Lewis; *Geiriau Doeth* 'Cydymdeimlad', Dic Jones.

Gwasg Gee: *Caduynau yn y Meddwl* 'Mae Gennyf Freuddwyd Heddiw', Gwyn Thomas; *Tantalus* 'Yfory', Caradog Prichard; *Yr Haf a Cherddi Eraill* 'Cysur Henaint', R. Williams Parry.

Y Lolfa: *Y Casgliad Answyddogol* 'Codi'r Caead', Derec Tomos.

Gwasg Christopher Davies: *Y Casgliad Cyflawn* 'Yr Einioes', 'Gormod', J. M. Edwards.

Llywodraeth Cynulliad Cymru 'Addewid ar Ddiwrnod Cofio'r Holocost', Gwyneth Lewis.

Gan yr awduron unigol: 'O Lili Wen Fach', Aled Gwyn; 'Desiderata', Bethan Mair; 'Cariad', Desmond Healy; 'Gwreiddiau', 'Dadeni', Mererid Hopwood; 'Os', Owen R. Hughes, (Dewi Hughes); 'Priodas', 'Gweddi', 'I'm Cydnabod', Dic Jones; 'Mesur Dyn', John Gwilym Jones; 'Gweddi'r Terfyn', Saunders Lewis, (Mair Saunders Jones); 'Eirlys', Gwynfil Rees, (Delyth Lewis); 'I'm Hanwylyd', John Roderick Rees; 'Y Daith', Idris Reynolds; 'Cofio Catrin', Cen Williams; 'Y Canol Llonydd Distaw', Steve Eaves.